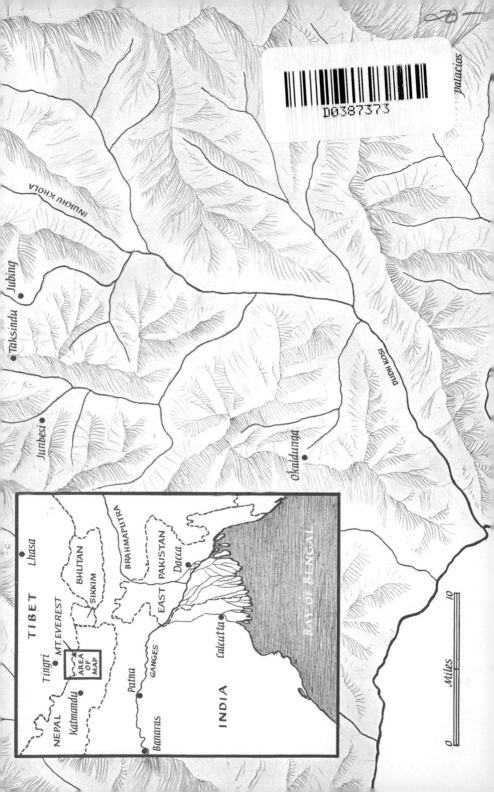

INUKHU KHOLA

Jubing

Taksindu

Junbesi

Okaldunga

DUDH KOSI

palacios

TIBET

Lhasa

BHUTAN

SIKKIM

BRAHMAPUTRA

EAST PAKISTAN

Dacca

BAY OF BENGAL

Tingri

MT. EVEREST

AREA OF MAP

Katmandu

NEPAL

Patna

GANGES

Calcutta

INDIA

Banaras

Miles

0   10

SCHOOLHOUSE IN THE CLOUDS

PREVIOUS BOOKS

HIGH ADVENTURE. The story of the climbing of Mount Everest in 1953

EAST OF EVEREST. An account of the New Zealand Alpine Club Himalayan Expedition to the Barun Valley in 1954 (with George Lowe)

THE CROSSING OF ANTARCTICA. The Commonwealth Trans-Antarctic Expedition 1955–58 (with Sir Vivian Fuchs)

NO LATITUDE FOR ERROR. Sir Edmund Hillary's personal story of his participation in the Trans-Antarctic Expedition

HIGH IN THE THIN COLD AIR. The story of the Himalayan Expedition led by Sir Edmund Hillary (1960–61), sponsored by World Book Encyclopedia (with Desmond Doig)

SCHOOLHOUSE IN THE CLOUDS

by Sir Edmund Hillary

Garden City, N.Y.

DOUBLEDAY & COMPANY, INC.

1964

ENDPAPER MAP BY
RAFAEL PALACIOS

PREFACE

The Himalayan Schoolhouse Expedition 1963 was an expedition with a difference. We planned to assault two great unclimbed peaks, members of the party were mountaineers of wide repute, yet our major program involved much more than this. We intended to repay in some measure the debt we owed to the Sherpas who live in the shadow of Mount Everest: we would build schools for them, pipe fresh water, and treat their diseases.

The name Sherpa does not mean mountaineer, guide or porter—it is simply the name of a race of people, Tibetan in origin, who inhabit the southern flanks of the Himalayan range. They are good and bad, strong and weak, honest and dishonest like the rest of us. But few of those who visit them can remain indifferent to their loyalty, affection and charm, or unimpressed with their remarkable toughness and courage.

It is to three of these Sherpas that I would dedicate this book:

> Mingmatsering   (Khunde)
> Angtemba   (Khumjung)
> Pembertarkay   (Phorche)

EDMUND HILLARY

CONTENTS

ILLUSTRATIONS

Chapter 1

"OUR CHILDREN HAVE EYES
BUT STILL THEY ARE BLIND!"

SHIVERING a little in the cold, we huddled around the smoky scrub fire. There were Urkien and Annullu, half a dozen other Sherpas, and three or four members of the expedition. It wasn't a pleasant campsite, here on this barren windy hollow beside the Tolam Bau glacier, but we hardly noticed. For hours we had been engrossed in a discussion about the history of the Sherpa people—and their future— in a broken mixture of Nepali and English. Every now and then Desmond would slip into fluent Nepali to clarify a point. The flames sank lower and the cold crept in around us. Urkien took a handful of stunted azalea and threw it on the fire. It flared up with a crackle of sparks and threw into relief the bearded, restless faces of the sahibs and the strong, poised countenances of the Sherpas against the desolate background of our 16,000-foot campsite.

In a warm flood of memory I dwelt on the many things we had gained over the years from our Sherpas. Not only help in the physical sense—so many loads carried here, so many risks taken there, or so many lives (alas) lost somewhere else. But few of us had failed to learn something from the character and temperament of the men themselves —their hardiness and cheerfulness, their vigor and loyalty, and their freedom from our civilized curse of self-pity.

"Tell us, Urkien, if there were one thing we could do for your village, what should it be? I know you would like a medical clinic and believe that your farms could be improved. But if you had one choice what would it be?"

"We would like our children to go to school, sahib! Of all the things you have, learning is the one we most desire for our children. With all respect, sahib, we know you have little to teach us in strength and toughness. We do not envy you your restless spirits—perhaps we are happier and more content than you are? But knowledge for our children—that we would like to see!"

This conversation took place in October 1960. In June of the following year four of us remained behind at the conclusion of our major expedition objectives to build the first school in the village of Khumjung—at 13,000 feet on the flanks of Khumbila, the sacred mountain, only a dozen miles from the foot of Mount Everest. The school had been made possible by a grant of $9000 from the expedition sponsors, World Book Encyclopedia. The ideal form of school building for these regions would be a modification of the robust Sherpa dwelling to give much more light but still retain the better features of Sherpa and Tibetan architecture. However, our expedition program had been a full one and we didn't have the time that such a structure would demand. Instead we compromised on a typically Western design—a 40×20-foot prefabricated aluminum building.

Some of the corrugated sheets for this building were 10 feet long and would have been virtually impossible to carry overland from Katmandu, the nearest city, 170 miles away. The Swiss Red Cross with their Pilatus Porter aircraft came to our rescue. They flew the hut sections into the hazardous mountain airstrip we had constructed at 15,500 feet in the Mingbo Valley. From there we carried them the day's march to Khumjung, and in a full week of vigorous effort assembled the complete building—a shining newcomer to the Sherpa scene but one which blended surprisingly well into the landscape.

From Darjeeling we recruited Tem Dorje Sherpa—a

schoolteacher of long experience with a competent grasp of the Nepali, Sherpa, Hindustani, and English languages. With a background in religion, customs, and language similar to that of his pupils and their parents, it seemed likely he would fit well into the pattern of local village life.

And so it proved. Over the next year reports kept coming in of the fine work Tem Dorje was doing and how successful the Khumjung School was proving to be. Perhaps the greatest compliments were the petitions from other villages nearby—villages like Thami.

27th October 1962

Sir

Respected Bara Sahib
Sir Edmund Hillary

We the local people, the Sherpas of Thami, Khumbu, came to know that your honour, helping us in all respects, is going to open some more schools in Khumbu. So we Thami people are requesting your honour to open a school at Thami just like Khumjung. *Though our children have eyes but still they are blind!* So all we Sherpas of Thami are praying your honour to make our children just like those in Khumjung. We hope your honour may consider our prayer.

Yours,
Chewang Rimpi Sherpa
Thak Noori Sherpa
Kinken Kung Sherpa
Khunjo Chumbi Sherpa

Over the years I have observed foreign aid programs in India, Nepal and elsewhere. Massive aid projects are essential where there are massive problems to be overcome. Yet too often they do little to create goodwill among the local people and frequently lead to an increase in cynicism, corruption and all the less desirable habits.

Until quite recently, for instance, a visitor to Nepal might well have been forgiven if he had gained the impression from the local newspapers that the United States of America was one of Nepal's major enemies and that this great country's motives warranted the most careful scrutiny. Few editions missed bitter comment on the high percentage of aid money that was being spent in transporting, housing and keeping American personnel. The vast amount of money going into useful programs, and indeed indirectly into the pockets of the critics, received scant and suspicious acknowledgment.

This attitude can be better understood if one reviews the early years of American activity in Nepal. When their aid commenced in the early 1950s Katmandu was a singularly isolated city with no road or air connections to the outside world. Entry permits were difficult to obtain, visitors had to walk or ride for a day and a half over a steep stretch of hill country. Freight was either carried over this track or swung high above the valleys on unsafe and temperamental cables. The few automobiles in Katmandu had been carried to the city over the same narrow track—with sixty-four porters per car. The city had electricity of sorts and a water supply, but both were notoriously erratic. Nobody bothered too much about these matters—the rich might have more light bulbs in their palaces than the poor, but they were all equally dim; and half a dozen water taps that won't work are no better than one if you're thirsty.

With American aid this fatalistic but contented acceptance of one's lot started to change. For the first time the ordinary Nepalese could see for himself what wealth really meant. The homes of the aid personnel weren't as big as the rana's palaces but they were much newer, and at night they had a brilliance never before seen in this unsophisticated valley. With massive logistic thoroughness the Americans had transported great diesel-electric generators for each house, and the steady thump of their motors reverberated about the quiet valley. It was a simple matter to pick out the American homes in the community—their lights shone clear and bright, seemingly unaffected by human frailty or mechanical weaknesses. The American homes didn't have as many servants as the rana's palaces, but they did have a lot and they always paid them—a precedent that rocked the local economy to its core.

Most of the early aid personnel were well-meaning enough, but many were unsuited to such a pioneering task. One genial old gentleman confided to me at a party in his very comfortable home that he hoped he'd be kept on in Katmandu, as he'd come out of retirement to accept the job and was far too old to get any further work back in the States. Several others frankly admitted that the generous salaries, allowances and taxation benefits were the main attraction. They were using their spell of duty to build up a useful financial nest egg. While there is nothing wrong about such attitudes in themselves—we all seek security and an opportunity to save—the basic feature of all aid work is that it should be creative. Aid work demands a pioneering spirit, an ability to adapt and improvise, an enthusiasm for people, and a readiness to put up with a certain degree of discomfort if this should prove necessary.

Slowly and painfully we are seeing world-wide acceptance of the fact that the wealthier and more technologically advanced countries have a direct responsibility to help the undeveloped ones—not only through a sense of charity, but also because only in this way can we ever hope to see any permanent peace and security for ourselves.

The importance of goodwill is frequently overlooked or ignored. We should not expect people to be continuously grateful for what is being done for them—the giver-receiver relationship is always a tricky and dangerous one, and most aid is strongly flavored with self-interest. Whereas gratitude has something of inequality about it, goodwill is an active and growing idea that a proud man need not feel ashamed to entertain. One of the most successful creators of goodwill in recent years has been the American Peace Corps. Few of the general public in an undeveloped country have any

personal contact with the money or the architects of an aid
project, but through organizations such as the Peace Corps
they can at last obtain a direct personal relationship. With
worth-while motivation, the volunteers live simply in town
and village, learn the local language, work with their hands
and minds alongside the local people, and at the same time
build up a fund of goodwill that does much to counteract
the side effects of more grandiose projects.

The basic fact is that *people* create goodwill—money cannot do it on its own. An excellent example of this is the
"Swiss" dairy in Katmandu. This dairy treats the milk for
most of Katmandu and is a worthy project indeed. The
funds and equipment for the dairy were donated by the
New Zealand Government under Colombo Plan, but an enthusiastic and hard-working Swiss manages the concern, so
it is called locally the "Swiss" dairy and creates much goodwill for the Swiss as a result.

Money is frequently the easiest thing for a country to
give. Trained personnel are chronically short even in the
more highly developed countries. Yet they are absolutely
vital in a land that is trying to leap from the Middle Ages
to the twentieth century in a decade. Nepal is already receiving a great deal of assistance both from the West and
from the communist world. Some of these programs are
imaginative, some are premature or have been given un-
necessarily high priority. The countries working in Nepal
range from Britain, which has had the most out of Nepal
through the employment of the famous Gurkha troops,
among the finest warriors in the world, (and which propor-
tionately has put much less back into the country); the
smaller countries such as Switzerland, which has a number
of practical projects, to America, Russia, China and India
whose giant programs seem forced to compete with each
other in this strategic mountain kingdom. Much of this aid
is being devoted to the Katmandu Valley and the Terai
area, which contain the greater centers of population.

Three days' walk into the hills and life goes on much as it has for a century. On the long border with Tibet little Western aid has yet penetrated. Here amongst the Sherpas the Chinese invasion of Tibet is still described in hushed and horrified tones, but with much less feeling than before. Time seems to be healing even the memories of the many refugee lamas in the monasteries, as it has healed their bodies. And everywhere the Sherpas shake their heads in admiration of watermelons being grown in Lhasa and the new schools which reports say the Chinese are building on the Tibetan highlands.

The Objectives

The districts of Solu and Khumbu in Nepal embrace the south side of Everest and its surrounding peaks and are the heart of the widespread Sherpa communities of eastern Nepal. The many villages are situated at altitudes of 7,000 to 14,000 feet. People subsist on an agricultural and pastoral economy. The Khumjung village school was the first such aid project in the Solu Khumbu and it had a substantial impact—but much more help was needed. I therefore resolved to organize further aid to the Sherpas. The Himalayan Schoolhouse Expedition 1963 was the result. My main motivation was the deep affection and respect I had developed for the Sherpas over many years of Himalayan expeditions, but there were other reasons. I was not unaware, for instance, of the increased penetration by Chinese Communist propaganda and money across the border and felt that the Sherpas should at least have some opportunity to see that Western society has its virtues and its opportunities for growth and freedom.

My plans for 1963 included a number of objectives. The most important was to build schools in the villages of Thami and Pangboche, situated an easy day's walk on either side of Khumjung. Then there were plans to pipe a fresh water supply to the villages of Khumjung and Khunde, and for the two expedition doctors to establish a clinic in Khumjung for six months to give general treatment to any sick people in the area. Finally I had a mountaineering program, an attempt on two of the most formidable peaks in the Everest area: the unclimbed summits of Mounts Taweche, 21,465 feet, and Kangtega, 22,340 feet.

The Sherpas have given much to Himalayan mountaineering and the mountains have given much to them in return. Not only have expeditions supplied a valuable source of income for the villages, but they have given the young men the chance to produce their finest qualities of courage and fortitude. Small aid projects such as mine have grown out of comradeship developed on the mountains. For these reasons as well as my own personal affection for the great peaks, I will always try to include an unclimbed summit in any expedition I may organize.

The Money

Finance is the major hurdle for an expedition. I estimated the 1963 program would cost approximately $54,000, but I also wanted to ensure that sufficient funds were put aside to guarantee the operation of the schools for at least a further three years. Mr. Bailey K. Howard, the chairman of Field Enterprises Educational Corporation, publishers of World Book Encyclopedia, agreed to sponsor the expedition once again. In a widespread campaign within this very large company (over 50,000 employees) a total sum of $52,000 was raised from the salespeople, the managerial staff, and the company itself. Of this, $14,000 was put aside for the maintenance of the schools and teachers' salaries up until 1966.

Those people who casually brush aside American generosity by saying, "Oh well, they can well afford it," have little real experience of the ordinary American in his own environment. He may have his weaknesses, but lack of sympathy for a worthy cause or reluctance to give freely are not among them.

Another Chicago-based corporation, Sears Roebuck and Company, also contributed substantially to the expedition. I am the adviser on camping equipment to this immense company which, among other reasons for fame, probably sells more tents and sleeping bags than any other retailer in the world. Sears Roebuck not only donated a number of tents and a large quantity of camping equipment, but also raised $10,000 for a film of the expedition's activities. The balance was obtained through sundry donations and by the sale of press rights, book rights, and European film rights. No expedition ever has sufficient financing, and certainly no expedition leader can afford to forget for long his budgetary problems. But for me this expedition was the least worrying financially I have undertaken.

I am occasionally asked, "What do you or the expedition members make out of an expedition?" The majority of the expedition members donate their time and energy in return for the opportunity to go to a region they have always dreamed of visiting, the culmination of ambition for any enthusiastic mountaineer. Two of the members could not afford to go unless they had some help with finances, and as their experience was valuable to me I gave them a modest subsidy. As for myself? I obtain part of my income from Field Enterprises and part from Sears Roebuck for work I carry out for them, but nothing directly from the expedition itself. In fact, as expedition banker I found myself mortgaging my credit to get the expedition clear of Nepal, for money from films and books is often not available until well after the conclusion of the trip.

The Men

In selecting members of the expedition, I looked for certain qualities. Desmond Doig, thirty-eight, who had played such a valuable part in the construction of the Khumjung School in 1961, was keen to go again. Desmond's grasp of the Nepali language and his ability to create close relationships with the Nepalese villagers were an invaluable contribution to such an expedition as ours. I am not good at languages. Although over the years I have acquired sufficient basic vocabulary to issue instructions or ask simple questions, this is not enough when dealing with village projects. Here Desmond came into his own—his is so adept an interpreter that many of the discussions reported in this book were channeled through him, and it almost seemed to me at the time that I was talking directly to the people concerned. Artist, writer, linguist, and humanitarian, Desmond is an astonishing character and life is never mundane when he's around. Every day produces a series of new enthusiasms and new crises, but nothing changes Desmond's unwavering affection for the mountain peoples of the Himalayan region.

We needed men who combined construction ability with a wide experience in technical mountaineering. To supervise our construction program we needed a competent and practical engineer. I therefore invited Murray Ellis, thirty-six, from New Zealand, to join the party. Murray is an experienced mountaineer and I had personal knowledge of his other formidable qualities, for he had spent fifteen months with me in the Antarctic in 1956–58. There Murray was base construction and maintenance officer and did an outstanding job. He was also a member of my five-man party which first took tractors overland to the South Pole. Immensely strong and energetic, Murray was at his best when the pressure was at its greatest.

The two doctors were Michael Gill, twenty-five, and Phillip Houghton, twenty-five, both from New Zealand. Mike Gill was by now a Himalayan traveler of wide experience, for he'd lived in the Everest region for ten months during my Scientific and Mountaineering Expedition 1960–61. A brilliant climber, Mike had been a member of the team on the first ascent of the formidable Ama Dablam, and he could be expected to go very well indeed at high altitudes. This was Phil Houghton's first visit to the Himalayas. Of powerful, chunky build, he had carried out many great climbs with Gill in New Zealand. Phil, a good practical physician, was to shoulder the onerous task of expedition doctor.

Tom Frost and Dave Dornan were from the United States. They were both twenty-six years old and had worked on construction and building jobs during their undergraduate years. Dave Dornan had an excellent mountaineering record in the Teton area of Wyoming and had done a difficult new route on 20,000-foot Mount McKinley, highest peak in North America. Dave was getting a master's degree in philosophy at the University of Colorado. My first contact with Tom Frost was rather an impressive one. He drove 830 miles for an interview, spent twenty minutes with me, and then quite cheerfully turned around and drove 830 miles home again. Tom was an aeronautical engineer and was regarded as one of America's most skilled rock climbers. Included in his record were several new routes on the 3000-foot rock cliffs of El Capitan in Yosemite Valley. I anticipated we would gain much value from Tom's technical skill if the rock cliffs on Taweche proved to be as steep as they looked.

We had a good all-rounder in Jim Wilson, twenty-six, from New Zealand. Jim had a master's degree in philosophy and a Commonwealth Fellowship to the University of Banaras to take his doctorate in comparative religion. Extremely muscular and craggy, Jim didn't particularly look like the ordained minister of the Presbyterian Church which he was. This was his first visit to the Himalayas, but he had behind him a long record of difficult climbs in New Zealand and the Antarctic. Of a cheerful, redoubtable temperament, Jim could be relied on to be a "whiz" on anything we undertook.

The nine-man team was completed with an Indian member, Bhanu Bannerjee, twenty-four. Bhanu was from Bengal and had been with me on the 60–61 expedition. He was an excellent interpreter in Nepali and had a pleasant and cooperative personality. Bhanu was still limping a little from frostbite incurred a short time before, when he had been one of the summit party of the first all-Bengal expedition to climb a 21,000-foot peak.

The Materials

Our equipment list took careful compiling. We needed several complete sets of carpenter's tools together with spades, shovels, pickaxes, crowbars and sledge hammers for earth moving and general construction. We intended using the basic Sherpa rock structure for our buildings, but carried in with us 160 sheets of corrugated aluminum 6 feet long for roofing. A dozen large windows were also transported (with mixed success) plus a new departure in these regions—a dozen sheets of corrugated Fiberglas to go into the roofs as skylights. The Alkathene plastic pipe for the water supply was made up into huge rolls weighing 60 pounds each, and these together with the roofing materials made up the most cumbersome and difficult loads for our porters.

In order to obtain the large quantities of local timber we would need for our buildings we had made some prepara-

1. Six-foot-long corrugated aluminum sheeting being carried from Banepa to Khumjung

2. Traditional scarves extend Khumjung's welcome

3. Tem Dorje, headmaster

4. The schoolhouse gleams as brightly as when first built

5. Small pupils with a great passion for learning

6. Khumjung School gathers for its official portrait

7. Tibetan acrobatic dancing

HIGHLIGHTS OF SPORTS DAY

8. Bobbing for sweet cakes

9. A spirited tug of war

tions in advance. I had met Sirdar Mingmatsering in Katmandu in December 1962 and had given him money and instructions to order timber and rocks. Although only a small amount of this timber had been accumulated by the time we reached Khumbu, yet at least it had given the villagers time to get used to the whole idea and become adjusted to donating their time and energy to laboring on the site.

Food wasn't too difficult a problem for us. I have become increasingly convinced of the value of using large quantities of local foods to supplement our diet. Judging by the voracious appetites of the party, this worked very successfully. From overseas I had brought such basic foods as dried milk, tinned butter, chocolate, coffee, oatmeal, jams, bacon, canned fruit and dried soups. In India and Katmandu we obtained our biscuits, sugar, ghee (cooking fat), tea, dhal (split peas), nuts, chili peppers and curry. And in Nepal itself we purchased rice, flour, cheese (from a Swiss cheese factory), eggs, chickens, potatoes, tsampa (cooked ground barley) and dahi (curds). Fresh meat is always difficult to obtain after the winter when the animals are thin and scraggy. I had instructed Mingmatsering to purchase four yaks and twelve sheep in December, when they were readily obtainable, and feed them up over the winter. This he did and we had good meat all through our expedition. Yak meat, in particular, is first-class from a young animal and quite economical at Rs 250 per beast ($33). Our general menu was as follows:

Wake up:
  Tea or coffee, sugar, milk
  Sweet biscuits
Breakfast:
  Oatmeal, sugar, milk (alternating with hot cakes and maple
    syrup 1 day out of 3). Fried or scrambled eggs with fried
    potatoes
  Chapatties, butter, marmalade, honey, jam
  Tea or coffee, sugar, milk

On the march:
Chocolate, biscuits, lemon drink
Static Lunches:
Soup
Boiled potatoes
Biscuits, butter, jam, honey
Cheese and nuts
Tea or coffee, milk, sugar
Dinner:
Soup
Curried chicken stew and rice
or Roast chicken and roast potatoes
or Roast mutton or yak, plus potatoes
or Mutton stew and boiled potatoes, etc.
Tsampa and dahi
or Canned fruit
or Dried apricots and custard
or Jello

The mountaineering objectives would not require a series
of camps at extreme altitude, so I didn't bother with a pre-
packed assault ration—which is rarely wholly successful in
any case, due to personal idiosyncrasies about food. Instead
I brought large quantities of excellent freeze-dried meats
and stews. Out of our bulk supplies a balanced diet was
sorted into polythene bags sufficient for the particular need
—biscuits, butter, honey, jam, chocolate, milk, sugar, lemon
powder, tea, coffee, dried soups, porridge, canned fruit,
sardines, cheese, and so on.

We used four assault tents (two Mead and two Blan-
chard) on the mountain, but the remainder of the tents
were standard camping types supplied by Sears Roebuck—
and very comfortable and successful they were. In fact the
new two-man pack tents were the best camping tents I had
used and they became so popular that they were selected
by choice for all occasions up to 17 and 18,000 feet on
Taweche and Kangtega. On the march you can always ex-

pect a lot of rain in the premonsoon season, and it's a blessing to have an ample supply of tarpaulins. We had half a dozen 15×20-foot tarpaulins, which proved to be mighty useful for protecting both men and material.

The major problem in establishing an aid project in the Khumbu region is its isolation from Katmandu. Even to make a quick check of progress in the schools becomes a large undertaking, involving a month of travel and considerable logistic effort. For this reason I toyed with the idea of building an airfield at Chaunrikharka, a day's march below Khumjung. I wrote to a large American aircraft company suggesting that they might like to lend the expedition an aircraft for the duration of our program. I was turned down—but in as cheerful a manner as I have ever experienced.

"Our Company President has asked if my budget would allow any kind of proposal to you. You are, without a doubt, the best known and most respected man in your field and I hope our product can serve you, not only on your presently proposed expedition in February, 1963, but on your future expedition. I do not, however, feel that I can do this from my budget—we must, of course, look for a return on publicity, and although I recognize there can be a picture now and then showing the airplane in use it can in no way be a feature.

"I do not know how intimately you are acquainted with our early American history, but during the time we refer to as The American Revolution our people in the Boston—Cambridge area were warned of a pending attack through a night ride by Paul Revere on a horse. This is a part of all of our official history books and a part of many sayings, poems, songs, etc. There is a saying in our country that everyone knows the name of Paul Revere, but no one knows the name of his horse. I feel this describes our position in regard to furnishing an airplane from our publicity budget."

In the end I decided with reluctance that we didn't have
the finances or time to carry out this project and delayed it
to another year and another expedition.

The Customs of the Country

By the end of February the expedition supplies were con-
verging on Calcutta from various corners of the globe. Then
commenced that most trying of all expedition periods—the
clearing of supplies through the Indian and Nepalese customs. In Calcutta's sticky heat we labored mightily to
hasten the formalities and complete documentation. Indian
customs regulations are not designed for the quick transit
of goods, and our frantic efforts to hasten the routine were
met with a somewhat jaundiced eye. In 1960 we had been
asked to guarantee a bond equivalent to the duty payable
on expedition equipment—a bond which was released when
we produced proof that all the gear had been either re-
exported or consumed. On this basis I had made arrangements for the bank to cover us up to a total of $12,000. I
now made the unpalatable discovery that the Indian customs had recently changed their policy. To the total value
of the expedition supplies we had to add 20 per cent to
cover insurance and freight. This made $16,000. But we
weren't going to get off this lightly—we were advised that
one guarantee wasn't enough. I had to have two of them—
one to ensure the equipment was exported out of India into
Nepal and one to ensure it was exported out of Nepal and
out of India again. So for expedition equipment worth about
$13,400 we had to guarantee $32,000 in duty. For a while
I wondered if our plans were to founder in Calcutta.

A patient and long-suffering bank manager made the expedition possible again. "Oh, that's all right," he said. "We'll
sign the guarantee for you. By the time you get back the
policy will have changed anyway." He was absolutely

right. By the end of the expedition the policy *had* changed and the Indian Government had conceded that only one bond equivalent to the value plus 20 per cent should be sufficient to cover the equipment on its movements both into and out of India. (Six months after the conclusion of the expedition we still hadn't obtained final release of our two bonds.)

On Tuesday March 5 most of our supplies flew into Katmandu in a chartered DC-3—not the cheapest but certainly the easiest way of getting anything into Nepal. Clouds were writhing around the hills and we had no view of the mountains, but Katmandu itself was washed fresh and clean by the rain. My reception by the government officials at the Singha Durbar was cordiality itself. The necessary permits were made final in record time. Unfortunately this cooperation hadn't penetrated into the lower echelons of the customs department, and we experienced the usual series of frustrations and tribulations before our equipment was all stamped and cleared. Perhaps I can blame myself for this —I have always been loath to join the "something for the boys" school but am coming to the weak view that in the long run it is the cheapest and easiest way out.

Sorting and issuing of equipment and its packaging into 60-pound loads is a busy time for everyone, but it's good fun all the same. The process is rather like all your Christmases coming at once—box after box of new clothing, shiny, unused equipment, enough groceries to fill a country store, plus the pleasure of meeting so many old friends again: Sirdar Mingmatsering, Angtemba, Pembertarkay, Pangboche Tenzing, Siku, Hakpanurbu Kunde, Phudorje—as redoubtable a group of Sherpas as you'd ever find together. The weather was pleasantly cool most of the time and we enjoyed the vigorous exercise of lumping about boxes, bales, kitbags, and bundles. One day we were engulfed by the most vigorous hailstorm I have ever experienced. Hailstones 1/2 to 3/4 inch in diameter were dropping onto us (the largest we measured was 1¼ inches in diameter) and we feared for our tents. Three or four inches of hail fell before the storm had passed. Our tents sagged under the weight, but were unaffected.

Next morning was clear and sharp and we had a magnificent view of the mountains, clothed in fresh snow to very low levels and looking incredibly beautiful. We seemed to get a new spurt of energy from the view and worked like madmen all day. In the evening we were entertained by the third prince and did full justice to delicious Nepalese food amid sophisticated surroundings—the last we would experience until the end of the expedition.

On March 12 we loaded all of our equipment into three trucks and drove out to the end of the road at Banepa. The mountains were sharp and clear, a thrilling sight. We were bemused with everything we saw—the mountains, the paddy fields, the pretty Nepali farmhouses, the smiling faces, and the stocky, capable figures of our Sherpas. Within two hours we had issued loads to 200 porters, said our goodbyes to our friends, and swung out along the path towards our first night's camp. All day the mountains beckoned us and we plowed on, intoxicated by their beauty.

Chapter 2

WATER FOR KHUMJUNG

Our welcome in Khumjung was heartwarming. We had climbed the hill from Namche Bazar in a haze of chang (beer) and rakshi (spirits) forced on us by Sherpa friends and by the captain in charge of the checkpost. Coming over the crest of the pass, we saw that most thrilling of all views—Taweche, Everest, Ama Dablam, Kangtega and Tamserku in a fantastic semicircle of impossible-looking summits. All the high country was under a heavy mantle of snow and winter seemed barely behind us.

From the Buddhist chorten on the pass we dropped down a steep rocky stairway winding between stunted pine trees and twisted rhododendrons clustering around the feet of giant moss-covered erratic boulders. A hundred feet below we came to a subsidiary pass and caught our first glimpse of the village of Khumjung—a scattering of solid-rock houses under the snow-draped buttresses of Khumbila. A few more steps and Khumjung School came into view, gleaming in the sun and looking as bright and new as ever. It brought back vividly our departure from Khumjung just under two years before.

We descended the last rock steps and ducked under the ancient extrance arch to the village. Schoolmaster Tem Dorje, with beaming face, was here to greet us and conduct us under a second arch of leaves and branches draped in prayer flags and with a large "Welcome" inscribed across the top. In something of a daze we passed down between two lines of excited children all shouting in English, "Welcome to Khumjung School."

Then we were hugging and thumping all our old Sherpa friends, many with tears unashamedly rolling down their cheeks—Khunjo Chumbi, who had been around the world with us, carrying the reputed yeti ("Abominable Snowman") scalp; Khunde Major, the senior headman; Ongchu Lama, who had played so important a part in the establishment of this first school; the rest of the village headmen and elders, all old friends of ours; the dignified senior Sherpanis and the young wives of our climbing Sherpas. It was a most emotional occasion.

We were led to the school, where a table groaned under the weight of food and drink. The women of the village placed around our necks the traditional *katas* (white scarves) and plied us with tea, chang and rakshi. There were speeches of welcome and a general hum of pleasurable excitement at this happy occasion. Every now and then another familiar face would swim out of the crowd to smile in welcome and then disappear.

The drinking and eating would have gone on indefinitely if we had allowed it, but there was still work to be done. Our coolies had unloaded in camp; they were now waiting to be paid off. In every shady spot there were snowdrifts and the temperature was dropping rapidly. The Tamang coolies weren't clad for this sort of climate and already were looking cold and miserable. We set up a table, brought out our bags of money and started paying off everyone against the books. To ensure that the porters left Khumjung with some food and drink inside them, I had ordered boiled potatoes and chang for 200 men. Each man received his pay and baksheesh and was then led aside to fill his bowl with soupy chang and be given a large handful of hot potatoes.

The daily rate for porters was six rupees, making a total of ninety-six rupees (thirteen dollars) for the sixteen-day march, less the advances already received. As well we paid baksheesh ranging from five rupees for an ordinary load to fifteen rupees for the more cumbersome ones—the rolls of Alkathene water pipe, corrugated aluminum sheeting, and bundles of windows. This is not high pay by Western standards, but a local merchant would give barely 50 per cent of this and his men would carry an extra 20 pounds as well. Some of our porters had been particularly useful or cheerful and were rewarded accordingly. One little old dwarf lady weighing 54 pounds had carried a 58-pound load all the way so I gave her an extra ten rupees, much to her delight —and the laughter of the crowd. By the time the last person was paid, the sun had long since departed and I was frozen stiff. We had a hasty meal and then, physically and emotionally tired, crawled into our warm sleeping bags.

What a pleasure it was to lie in next morning, even though the weather was fine and clear! There is a certain inevitableness about life when you're on the march, as we had been. It doesn't matter how you feel, you still have to get up and get going. A day's delay means 250 people are being paid for nothing, and this isn't to be considered. But now we could stretch out comfortably in our bags and look through the tent door at the hard frost covering the ground and bushes. Not till the warm sun touched our tents did we bother to stir.

Our first task was to establish a mess hut that would be reasonably comfortable over the three months we would be based on Khumjung. In the crisp air we worked vigorously, putting up a skeleton framework with long poles, then draping over it two of our large tarpaulins. I had brought with me several small wood-burning stoves (made in Katmandu out of oil drums) and we installed one of these in the mess hut. When it was glowing a cherry red, the hut became very cozy indeed; we spent many pleasant evenings here in bitter weather.

I snatched time off to make one diplomatic call—a meeting with the village headmen in the *gompa* (temple) where I explained my plans to them, seeking their approval of various projects. It was a convivial gathering and inevitably resulted in the production of brass-banded wooden chang bottles and dusty glass bottles filled with potent rakshi. Although I restricted my consumption to the bare minimum required by etiquette, I found even a minimal consumption of raw spirits in the morning impaired my efficiency for the rest of the day. Fortunately only Desmond and I needed to undertake these formal visits—the rest of the party carried on with the work at great speed. Murray and Jim spent all afternoon producing that most important of structures— a comfortable toilet. It was open to the sky, but at least concealed us from the curious gaze of any passer-by.

As Before—But with a Few Changes

I was delighted to find that Khumjung seemed as lovely as ever it had been. Too often our impressions of places improve with absence, but I had no need here to feel that I had been deluding myself. The enthusiastic comments of the expedition members making their first visit were proof enough in themselves even if my eyes had been closed. The crisp days and the heavy snow on the mountains added to the beauty. Spring was still a little way off and in shady places the ground was frozen hard all day. But the scattered snowdrifts were rapidly shrinking in the warm sun. Many of the houses in the village had received a face lift since our last visit nearly two years before. There was a bright air about the place with plenty of whitewashed walls and painted window frames, some even boasting windows of glass. All day long we were saying *"namaste"* (greetings) to the children going to and from school.

And what a change there was in the children—superficial, of course, but change none the less. Instead of faces and hands coated with years of dirt and soot, they were clean and glowed with the flush of perfect health; instead of dirty, torn clothing, their garments showed at least some attempt at tidiness and care. It was always a delight to visit the school and look at the children, there was such a passion for learning—none of the reluctance we accept as normal in our more sophisticated society. Already the children were displaying the natural intelligence we had always suspected was ready to be developed amongst the Sherpas. Tem Dorje was particularly proud of his brightest pupil. This boy had been unable to read and write two years before. Now he could read and write Nepali fluently, and Nepali was not his mother tongue. He could also read and write English with astonishing facility. After school hours you could walk through the village and see ample signs of the children's enthusiasm for their new education. Out of an open window would come drifting, childish voices practicing reading or learning arithmetic tables. Or you'd pass a couple of students sitting cross-legged in the field in front of their home, writing line after line of flowing Nepali with the dedication of any scholar.

We had put much thought into the problem of how far we should take the children along the path of education. Too much education could make the children misfits in the simple life of their community. They'd drift to the towns, joining the growing band of partly educated—those not well enough trained to get a good job but too proud to dirty their hands with physical labor. In reviewing the Sherpa way of life and estimating where Western knowledge could most profitably be used, I inevitably came back to the needs of public health and agriculture. As fewer people die from smallpox, malaria and TB and more mothers and babies come safely through childbirth, so the population will rise. And as the population rises so does the need for food. It is not easy to teach people to adopt new methods and ways of living if they are unable to read and write, so this seemed to us a first priority. Initially we didn't plan to take the children beyond the sixth-grade level. Only those few pupils who made outstanding progress would be given more education with a view to filling the need for more teachers.

The aluminum school building had stood up well to its two years of life. The only noticeable fault was a pronounced dip in the ridge produced by the weight of the exceptional snowfalls of the previous winter. The villagers told us that at one stage there had been three feet of snow packed on the roof, and this had proved too great a burden for the central truss. Murray Ellis tackled this problem with forceful determination. Wooden beams were cut from the local forest and fitted into place. With sledge hammer and levers the ridgepole was lifted back to horizontal and securely supported by a new wooden truss. When completed, it was all as good as new—better, in fact. Now it could withstand any conceivable weight of snow.

We had left a number of spare windows for the school, but found to our surprise that these had all been used. Tem Dorje explained in much wrath that vandalism is not lacking even in these mountain villages. During the cold winter months when the school was closed, "drunken Tibetans had thrown rocks at the windows just to see if they would break," he explained. And break they did! We had little confidence in any village *panchyat* (council) restricting such actions, so took our own measures. Out of rough-sawn planks we manufactured heavy wooden shutters so that the building could be well protected during the long winter. The smashing of the windows had not been completely innocent, we believed. We suspected that there were people in the Khumbu area who were jealous of the Khumjung School and afraid of the influence it might wield.

Our first major task in Khumjung was to improve the inadequate water supply. It was a perfect morning, sunny but cool, when a group of us set off to examine the water's source above the village. We followed the winding track through potato fields and then up the flanks of Khumbila to

the east of the village. Gaining steady height, we hiked
around a bald knob and entered a dry and rocky gully.
Three hundred and fifty vertical feet above the village we
came to the first sign of water—two seepage pools lined with
rock walls and covered with wooden beams weighted down
with rocks. Sitting patiently beside the holes were several
villagers with their wooden water casks and brass ladles. As
the water slowly seeped into the bottom of the holes, they
would scoop it into the casks. It was a most laborious business. We could easily believe the Sherpas' estimate that it
took over an hour to get a full load. This was too inadequate
a supply of water for our needs, so we carried on upwards.

The track climbed even more steeply now, first over two
narrow dry washes, and then across a boulder-strewn slope
peppered with stunted pine trees. Six hundred feet above
the village we dropped into another river bed, also dry and
arid, but above us we could hear the sound of splashing
water. We scrambled into a narrow canyon with smooth
rock walls and a trickle of water in the bottom. At its head
we came to an abrupt rock face with water tumbling down
it in a little waterfall. No great supply of water this—in a
hundred yards it disappeared into the shingle—but far more
than the village needed for drinking and washing.

We asked our Sherpas about this stream. Did it ever dry
up?

"Yes, sometimes, but not often. Then we climb higher and
higher up the mountainside until we find a trickle again."

"What happens in winter?"

"It freezes up, although there is usually some water running under the snow and ice. But in the winter we are not
troubled. We only need go outside our houses to the nearest
snowdrift."

"Does much water flow down here during the monsoon?"

"Yes, after heavy rains this stream carries a lot of water
and we use it to drive our water wheels for grinding the
grain. As you can see, we have made a little irrigation chan-

nel around the mountainside to try and bring the water closer to the village, but even in the monsoon it soaks away into the soil well before it reaches the village."

One solution would have been to dam up the canyon and make a storage lake. This was a task beyond our meager resources. Instead we planned a tiny buffer dam—enough to make a small pool at the foot of the waterfall, and from this we'd lead off our pipe down the hillside. It wasn't an ideal situation and would require supervision by the villagers, but it was the best we could do.

Stimulated by the brisk air and tremendous views, we carried on up the mountainside, across steep bluffs and up long tongues of snow. Our lungs were gasping for air at this unaccustomed altitude but we drove on, enjoying the fight and the pleasure of being back on a mountain again. We kicked steps up a last long snowslope to reach the crest of the ridge at 15,150 feet—and flopped down to rest on a dry warm patch of snow grass. Ahead of us the terrain dropped away abruptly for thousands of feet and, filling our whole horizon, was the massive south face of Taweche. We eagerly scanned it with the glasses, but the more we saw, the more uncompromising the whole mountain looked. The left-hand ridge was long and difficult with a tremendous vertical rock step in it. The south face itself was quite out of the question —a huge precipice swept by rockfall and ice avalanche. Only on the right-hand ridge could we see any prospect of success—and then only if we could first surmount an almost vertical 2000-foot rock buttress.

Somewhat subdued by the challenge the mountain presented, we dragged ourselves to our feet and plunged down the mountainside in wild disorder, glissading the snowslopes, sliding down the loose shingle in a cloud of rocks and dust, and pounding along the narrow yak trails. We reached the bottom flushed and breathless. Wasting no time, we half galloped over to the village of Khunde, for

Sirdar Mingmatsering was entertaining us all at lunch and already we were late.

With cautious glances at the snarling Tibetan mastiff watchdog, we entered Mingma's solid but unpretentious house and climbed up the dark stairway to the living quarters above. With warm dignity Mingma introduced us to his family and friends and then conducted us to the places of honor on the low carpet-covered bench against the wall. Then Mrs. Mingmatsering was putting glasses in our hands, pouring out a welcoming brew of chang. This was no ordinary chang—smooth and clear, it had been well matured in our honor and tasted like a good white wine. And then the food was brought by willing hands—omelet, rice and curry, boiled potatoes, and finally dahi (curds) with tsampa and sugar. Almost bursting with good food and drink, we had little inclination to do any work that afternoon.

A Trickle, a Flow

Khunde village is less than half a mile from Khumjung. It has only half the population, yet the headman of Khunde (the Khunde Major, as he is called) is the over-all headman of both villages. Khunde has its own meager water supply. Mingma was anxious for us to try to do something to improve it. We were shown several seepage pools near the village and marveled that two hundred and fifty-odd souls could survive from such a source. Each year these holes dried up, we were told, and then the villagers had to go half a mile up the valley to a spring which always had some water.

After our sumptuous lunch we made heavy weather of the climb up the valley towards a great towering rock marking the source of the spring. At the foot of the rock we found it: a faint trickle of water which seeped away within ten feet of its emergence. We looked at each other and shrugged our shoulders—what could we do with this? We'd have to dig around a bit to see if we could increase the flow enough for it to be worth piping down the valley, but we didn't like the look of the unstable mass of loose rock and mud overhanging the spring.

Next morning Murray Ellis and Jim Wilson returned to the Khunde spring with pickaxes, shovels, crowbar and a couple of strong Sherpas. All day they dug and poked, shoveling out tons of rubbish, prizing away boulders that threatened to crash on them from above, and slowly, very slowly, increasing the flow of the spring. By the end of the day they were getting about a gallon a minute—still a rather miserable trickle, but equivalent to over 1200 gallons in twenty-four hours. They made a little catchment pool lined with impermeable clay and led the water off with a short length of pipe into an open four-gallon tin. If this ran consistently for the next week or two, it would then be worth laying a pipe down the hill to the village.

As Jim shoveled in the dim, sloppy hole under the rock, he was startled to see an unexpected movement. He looked a little closer into the darkest corner and to his astonishment discovered a small frog sitting there, quite unconcernedly. What it lived on or how it survived he had no idea, but the thought that this might be some strange new species flashed across his mind—after all, frogs at 13,000 feet under hundred-ton boulders can't be too common. He carefully picked up the unresponsive creature and placed it in a cardboard box to bring down to base camp.

That evening we examined his find with great interest. It was Mingma, I believe, who first mentioned a possible complication in respect to the frog. This was undoubtedly the god of the spring, he pointed out. If it were harmed, the water might very well cease to flow. The rest of our Sherpas nodded their heads sagely and confirmed this view. "It would be wise to return the god, sahib," they said.

"What a terrible thing it would be for Khunde if the spring disappeared?" Poor Jim had been motivated only by a disinterested dedication to science, but now his frog had entered into the political and religious fields. He received advice from the expedition members: "You'd better hand-feed it, Jim"; "The frost tonight will kill it. You'd better keep the frog in your sleeping bag with you." There was certainly cause for concern, as the nights were cold and we had no idea what resistance a frog might have to a severe frost. Jim devoted himself to his task like a mother—he covered the frog's box with a warm cloth and placed it in the tent beside him. Various delicacies were offered to the creature (who refused them with disdain). Frequent examinations were made to see that it was still alive. A bleary-eyed Jim was vastly relieved in the morning to find the frog unaffected by its treatment. After breakfast he carried it back to the Khunde spring, and with all due ceremony placed it carefully in a dark corner under the rock. With serious mien the Sherpas nodded their heads in approval. "The god will be pleased, sahib, and the water continue to flow!" We never did find out whether our Sherpas were really serious or were just having a practical joke.

We decided to lay the water pipe to Khumjung in rough-and-ready fashion and then let it run for a while experimentally to uncover any problems. Murray, Jim, Dave and I plus a group of our Sherpas laden with the huge rolls of piping set off up the hill in the early morning. It was brilliantly clear—Tamserku and Ama Dablam seemed close enough to touch. As we laboriously climbed up to the water source, we left rolls of pipe strategically placed en route. The canyon was cold and still. Ice covered the rocks. Only a modest trickle of water was flowing down the waterfall, but the flow perceptibly increased as the warm sun went to work on the frost-bound slopes above. By 10 A.M. the water was splashing down in volume and the sun had penetrated even into the canyon. We threw ourselves at the rocky bed of the stream and built a rough dam behind which a small catchment lake rapidly accumulated. On the end of the pipe we attached a wire-netting cage to keep out the worst of the rocks, then we anchored it well down in the pool. The five-foot-diameter rolls were demons to handle in the chill air, but we rolled them down the mountainside, following the contours as best we could. Around the trees and rocks, down steep bluffs, over dry creek beds and through tight scrub we went. As each 140-yard roll was laid, we'd connect it to the one above and cheer enthusiastically as the water gushed out.

Murray joined the last roll and we yelled with joy as the water rushed out in a fine stream—6 gallons a minute or more. A couple of villagers were passing on their way up for water. They filled their water carriers with smiles of pleasure. A few children appeared, grubby and blackened as many of the Sherpa children are, and they needed no second invitation to wash themselves under the spurting pipe. Ignoring clothes and boots, they plunged their arms, their heads and bodies into the water.

Feeling like conquerors, we galloped down to camp for a late lunch. By the time we'd finished, it was snowing steadily. It usually did in the afternoon. This day happened to be one of the four days in the year on which the villagers did honor to the god Khumbila. The houses were all gay with new bright flags on the roofs and ceremonial fires burning in every courtyard. It was with difficulty, therefore, that Desmond and I were able to drag the village elders away from their celebrations and walk them up to see the new pipe. Everything was obscured by a veil of falling snow. My heart sank when I was unable to hear the sound of running water.

We came to the end of the pipe and the water was still there—flowing free and clear onto the snow-covered ground. The elders were quite overcome at the sight. Ongchu Lama jumped from one foot to the other, laughing quite uncontrollably; one elder just kept clapping his hands, while another stood with tears flowing down his cheeks. In great excitement they discussed the final location of the pipe, and the collecting tank we planned to build there. Then, in high good humor, we returned to the village with the elders and accepted their pressing invitations to join with them in the Khumbila celebrations.

All evening we were entertained in gay and lighthearted fashion. We bandied tales with old friends, drank much good chang, and watched vigorous Sherpa dancing; the air was full of song and laughter. All of my party were brought in to join us and partake of the food and drink. I can't remember a pleasanter evening or having felt more clearly that we were really being accepted into the Sherpas' hearts and lives. It was late when we finally said good night and stumbled our way homeward under a star-filled sky. A final culmination of the evening was our discovery that the mail runners had arrived, and candles burned late in many tents as we read letters from our families and friends.

Despite the celebrations of the night before, Murray, Jim and I were up early and walked up the hill to take a look at the pipeline before breakfast.

Not a drop of water was to be seen!

We trudged on up the hill, flexing the pipe and feeling ice inside it. When we reached the source in the canyon we found the first length of pipe and the collecting pool frozen solid. Only a bare trickle of water was coming down the waterfall. Our main error had been to have the first fifty feet of pipe almost horizontal without enough fall to keep the water rushing along—and so it had frozen up. We cleared the ice out of this pipe and got water through it, then worked our way down the mountainside, clearing each length as we went. At 9 A.M. we reached the bottom of the pipe and out tinkled a hundred feet of ice fingers, impelled by the growing water pressure behind. Soon the water was running again.

A decision had to be made on the final positioning of the pipe. Should we dig it into the ground with vast effort or lay it on a raised rock wall above the surface? The manufacturers had warned us that the Alkathene pipe had such high insulating properties that if it were underground and became frozen it could be weeks before it thawed out again. We decided to have the pipe aboveground, and accepted the fact that it would freeze every cold night. We would rely on the sun's melting it out each morning. This system would have the advantage that if there should be any break in the pipe, at least it could be found and repaired.

For another ten days we continued the experiments. Each morning the pipe was frozen but by 10 A.M. it was usually running again. I had constructed a temporary tank out of a large tarpaulin; each night this filled with water and kept the village going until the flow returned.

There was a fresh dusting of snow on the ground the morning we started rounding up the villagers to help with the permanent establishment of the pipeline. At first people were slow in appearing, but the numbers grew and before we finished we had over 160 Sherpa men and women to help us. In lightly falling snow we trudged up to the canyon and started to build a low rock wall to support the pipe. The ground surface was rough and uneven. We had to move thousands of rocks, and in places make deep excavations. The Sherpas worked like demons, but were in gay holiday mood, and the jokes and badinage brought gusts of deep-throated laughter. In two places we had to bridge dry washes with heavy logs 25 and 30 feet long, and the younger Sherpas performed miracles of strength in getting these up the mountain and into position. We took care to maintain the wall at an even gradient so there would be no dips in the pipe, and the work went ahead at a fast pace. By 4 P.M. everyone had worked himself out. We were a noisy and well-contented group as we trudged wearily down to the village that evening.

In the morning the work went on. The causeway was soon completed to the village outskirts, and we started on the major task of excavating the ground for two 1200-gallon collecting tanks. All the village elders took a hand in organizing this, and the result was absolute bedlam and chaos. Somehow the work went on at astonishing speed, and by the end of the day huge rocks had been moved and a vast hole dug.

The tanks proved to be a major undertaking. We had to improvise as best we could. First we employed stonemasons to build substantial rock walls. We had a little cement and so lined one of the tanks with wire netting, then plastered on an inch of concrete plaster. The second tank was plastered with local clay and lined with a plastic-coated nylon tarpaulin. It was a great day when the job was completed and we turned the water into the tanks to fill them to brimming. The village now had two days' reserve of water in case the pipe should block for any reason.

Khunde water supply proved a simpler task. The "god" of the spring bore no resentment at his harsh treatment, and the water kept trickling out. We laid half a mile of pipe down the mountainside to the seepage tank beside the village. Organized by Mingmatsering and the Khunde Major, every villager turned out to build a supporting wall over rocky slopes and steep gullies. When it was finished, the water flow was hardly impressive—only two gallons every three minutes—but every morning the seepage pool was full, something that had never happened before, and the Khunde water shortage was over.

Public Education in the Himalayas

Our establishment of the Khumjung School two years before had stimulated further educational activity in the Khumbu region. Two villages, Namche Bazar and Chaun-

rikharka, had opened schools with government grants of
Rs 900 per annum each ($120). The villagers had helped
as best they could, but the schools were maintaining a bor-
derline existence. Both of these villages approached me with
the suggestion that we take over their schools and finance
their operations. But of course it isn't feasible just to walk
into a government school, however inadequately financed it
may be.

Namche Bazar was less than an hour's walk and a thousand feet below Khumjung, so we saw a good deal of the
place. It is the administrative center of Khumbu and the
location of the Nepalese Military Check Post and radio.
This may sound an impressive setup, but such is not the
case. Due to its isolation from Katmandu, the checkpost is
usually composed of one officer and two or three soldiers.
None of these men is really at home in such a high and
rigorous climate; they suffer as well from being underpaid
and ill-equipped. The radio is a primitive contraption with
batteries charged from a pedal charger (two Sherpas are
employed to supply the necessary horsepower for battery
charging). If the radio breaks down it cannot be mended
on the spot—it has to be packed up and carried by a coolie
into Katmandu for repairs. By the time it returns, at least
a month has passed. The radio enables the Nepalese Government to keep a check on the Tibetan border, a mere
twelve or so miles away—or so the theory goes. In practice
Namche Bazar is so far from the border that it is easily
bypassed by anyone not wishing to be seen, and the radio
is so unreliable that it would have to be silent for at least
three weeks before the authorities in Katmandu felt the
slightest concern about it—and much can happen in three
weeks.

Namche Bazar itself is not one of the more attractive
Sherpa centers. Crammed into a tight hollow in the mountainside, it is appallingly dirty and dusty for the majority
of the year. Only when the monsoon brings a carpet of

green to the potato fields does the village have any beauty at all—although there are always cool clean ice peaks outlined against the southern sky. The people of Namche are largely traders (many of them wealthy), but some have performed notably on Himalayan expeditions. It is unfortunate that over the years the village has developed a reputation for dishonesty, deceit and banditry. The community is split by two strong factions, each warring against the other. There isn't much to choose between them.

The history of the school in Namche Bazar was not a happy one. Some years ago the villagers made an effort and formed a school committee. Funds were raised locally, a Nepalese teacher obtained, and parents signed up to pay fees for their children. Alas for this worthy effort. Within a few short weeks someone had absconded with the school funds. The parents proved reluctant to pay the fees and the poor teacher, ill-clad and hungry, retreated in disorder to Katmandu.

The next step in the Namche Bazar school saga was a gift of Rs 3500 toward a schoolhouse by the Indian Everest Expedition. This was a singularly generous gesture, and for this sum an excellent structure could be built. The government's annual Rs 900 was used to employ a teacher (this time a Sherpa). Classes were commenced.

The checkpost captain advised us that the village elders wanted us to visit their school so they could put certain proposals before us. Desmond Doig and I went down one afternoon to a rousing reception. I was most impressed by the numbers of well-dressed children outside, singing songs of welcome, and agreed that the school was a going concern. There was even a night class, it seemed, and fifteen lovely Sherpa maidens in their best finery were introduced to us as the star pupils. A large crowd of villagers had crammed into the schoolhouse and we went in to join them.

My first impressions of the school were disappointing. It was hard to be oblivious of the fact that half of the back wall had collapsed under the pressure of the winter snows. The building had no floor. We were forced to cross a stretch of sticky clay spotted with pools of water. The villagers were perched cheerfully on planks above the water level. The school had no glass in the windows, no books, no slates and no teaching equipment. It was quite obvious that nothing like Rs 3500 had been spent on the building. We suspected that most of that sum had been shared by some of the school committee.

Desmond and I were given places of honor and plied with tea and chang. Then the speeches started. First the teacher (a well-dressed and rather slick young man) spoke about how much they had done already and how eager they were to bring the school up to the standard of Khumjung. Then a village elder (plump and richly clad) spoke about the poverty of the village and how hard they found it to raise the money for improving the school. Desmond and I were impressed—so many children and young students were present and there seemed such a desire for improvement. First they must get the building into order, I said, and fix the gaping back wall.

"We intend to start on this in a few days' time. We have already raised the money for this," we were told.

"If some of the rich traders will donate the timber for the floor," I said with a fixed look at the plump gentlemen, "we will pay the wages of the carpenters to install it."

After a little discussion among the elders this too was agreed on. "As this is a government school," I pointed out, "we cannot take responsibility for it without government approval. However, I am prepared to help out with school equipment and books. If you make out a list of your requirements and bring it up to us at Khumjung, we will see what we can do." This offer was greeted with enthusiasm and we departed from Namche in a veritable spate of good wishes and appreciations.

It was eight more days before we heard anything from

10. As rolls of pipe are toted above Khumjung, Ama Dablam seems near enough to touch

11. Down steep bluffs, through tight scrub: Mingmatsering and Murray Ellis join two 140-yard rolls

12. Child watches over the result

13. Collecting tanks provide two days' reserve of water

14. Mingma and a young Sherpa share delight in the village fountain

15. Washing greens at the revolutionary water pipe

Namche except the infrequent rumor of dissension and strife between the two factions. Then one day the schoolmaster appeared and presented us with a long list of school requirements. The village council had met, he explained, and he had been appointed spokesman for them. He considered that their most urgent needs would be overcome if I donated Rs 1500 to the school. He would be happy to accept the money from me now so that work could be commenced at once. We glanced at the list and found it a most abstruse and unsatisfactory document. We started questioning the teacher closely. The more we asked, the more evasive he became. Our suspicions were now thoroughly aroused, and I resolved not to hand over the money meekly as requested —which I had no intention of doing anyway.

We had reached something of a stalemate when the teacher glanced with concern at the track from Namche and then hastily got to his feet, made mumbled excuses and headed off rapidly in the opposite direction. Five minutes later our camp was invaded by a new group from Namche —the members of the school committee. Nothing could surprise us now and only a few questions served to clear up some problems.

"No, there has been no meeting of the village council."

"No, we have made no list of requirements for the school and pupils."

"No, the teacher has no authority to collect money for the school. In fact we are planning to discharge him, as he is proving very difficult and we suspect him of dishonesty. Also he has been making love to the daughter of one of the richest men in the village."

Having disposed of the teacher, the school committee then set to work to persuade us once again to give substantial finance for the school operations. It didn't need the whispered advice of our own Khumjung Sherpas, telling us that this committee represented only one of the factions in the village, to help me make up my mind.

"We will make no agreements with any group in Namche! Return to your village! Arrange a meeting of the full village council, discuss the school and then send representatives to us for help and we will give it." Disappointed and subdued, the committee bowed and then departed.

The same afternoon we had a revealing discussion with one of the senior expedition Sherpas who came from Namche. We had noticed his two children at the Namche school reception and asked him how they were progressing with their schoolwork.

"But they don't go to school, sahib," he said in surprise. We explained that we had seen them at the Namche school. "That was nothing to do with going to school, sahib," he said. "On the day of your visit the school committee went all around the village explaining that in your honor all the children and young maidens must dress up in their best clothes and gather at the school for the function. This they did, and a fine ceremony it was. But of course no one went back to the school the next day."

We had no further deputations from Namche Bazar. The schoolmaster disappeared, taking the rich man's daughter with him; the wall of the school still gapes to the sky and the floor is a muddy lake. No children attend the school, there are no night classes, and education is at its customary standstill. The only ray of hope is that six children from Namche are now attending the Khumjung school. They are all children of leading village elders.

Namche Bazar is an influential and vital center in Khumbu. Through its trading contacts with Tibet and Katmandu it is a hotbed of subversion and underground activity. Government administration is almost negligible, due largely to its isolation (the most senior government official ever to have visited the Khumbu area was the police commissioner from Okaldunga). The only hope now for Namche, I believe, is for closer government administration, which could break up the local cliques and produce some sort of unity in the village. The Sherpas of Namche aren't too different from their relations in the surrounding villages, but they do need help with their internal problems. Perhaps a good school at Namche Bazar might supply the stabilizing influence that is so badly needed.

Chapter 3

EPIDEMIC

WE SAW our first smallpox in the tiny village of Surkya only two days' march from Khumjung. Approaching was a rather dignified-looking Sherpa woman, whose ragged clothes and lack of ornaments indicated she was poorer than average. She was a widow, she said, and her daughter was dying of smallpox. Would the sahibs visit her child and do what they could?

We had known there might be smallpox in the area. The American Everest Expedition had reported a case of the disease, and vaccine had been sent in to them. We received this news before we left Katmandu and as a precaution obtained from the World Health Organization representative in Katmandu a vaccination set sufficient for at least 200 people. Phil Houghton now searched through his medical supplies to find this vaccine and duly emerged with a neat little package. When he opened the package, his normally good-natured face suffused with anger—the vaccination set had already been used and was quite useless.

Phil, Desmond Doig and I set off across the fields with the distraught mother. None of our own Sherpas had been vaccinated so we instructed them to stay away. We entered a substantial but neglected Sherpa house, fumbled our way through the darkness of the lower floor and up the rickety stairway into the living quarters. All the shutters were drawn. It was dark and still, but I could see how terribly poor and empty the house was. At the far end of the room a quiet bundle lay on the floor, covered by a few rags. It was the daughter. The mother led us up to the sick girl and pulled back the clothes. It was with difficulty that I repressed a gasp of horror and pity. The rounded, comely face of this sixteen-year-old girl was covered with dreadful blisters and sores—and so was every inch of her body. One of her eyes was already blistered and lifeless, but the other watched us with desperate concentration.

I could see by the look on Phil's face that the case was virtually hopeless, but he examined the poor girl tenderly. The widow kept repeating, "She is dying! She is dying!" and we could tell from the girl's living eye that she understood. Desmond went into action.

Miracles have been achieved through faith, particularly amongst simple, uncomplicated people. In his fluent Nepali he assured the mother that the child would not die—that she had survived so long already that the worst was probably over . . . there was still hope and she must not give up so easily. When he had finished there was quiet for a while in the dingy room, but the weak breath of the girl, rasping through her blistered throat, was an ominous answer.

We were deeply concerned about the likelihood of the disease's spreading elsewhere in the village. "When the girl has recovered," said Desmond to the mother, "you must take her clothes and her blanket and burn them. Only by doing this can you stop the disease from spreading to your neighbors and friends."

"But what will my daughter wear—what will she sleep in? We have nothing else and I have no money."

"You must get some ointment for the girl's face to try to reduce the scarification," Desmond continued—and then stopped. How could they get ointment? They were terribly poor—the poorest Sherpas we had ever seen. I fumbled Rs 20 out of my pocket and thrust it into her unresisting hand. Phil gave her antibiotics to prevent any complicating infection and then we took our leave. It was good to be out in the fresh clean air again, but memories of the dying girl stayed with us for many days. We resolved that a vaccination program must become one of the major tasks of our expedition.

As we moved farther up the Dudh Kosi Valley we found a growing fear of smallpox. Already one had died in Surkya, and two more were dead in a village near Chaunrikharka. Many more were showing symptoms. The village panchyats (councils) pleaded with us to do what we could to stop the disease. At Namche Bazar we discussed the problem with the checkpost captain.

"You must send a message to the government over my radio," he said. "They wouldn't take any notice of me." A message was duly compiled and I suggested that the vaccine should be air-dropped to us at Khumjung. Two days later, with unprecedented alacrity, my request was granted when the Swiss Red Cross plane flew low over Khumjung and successfully dropped the vital parcels of vaccine. (Later I received a bill for Rs 800 ($105) for this mercy flight.)

By now we were receiving urgent messages indicating that the smallpox was spreading rapidly. We started our campaign in Khumjung and Khunde, and Phil Houghton soon had a cheerful, jostling crowd of men, women and children eagerly thrusting out their arms for treatment. The scratch method of vaccination is a simple procedure and before long Phil was supervising a mixed group of sahibs and our senior Sherpas, all taking a hand at the task. In the first twenty-four hours over 300 people had been vaccinated and, perhaps even more important, a group of us had become competent vaccinators. Then we started spreading our activities to the neighboring villages.

Our vaccine had come from two sources—Switzerland and Russia. The Russian proved potent, and there were few cases of its failing to "take" in a most vigorous fashion—in fact many people were so sick from it that they were convinced they were about to die. The Swiss vaccine must have been a bad batch. Although we tried every method we could, we were unable to get more than ten per cent of "takes." In one area we vaccinated 600 people twice without success and had to return a third time with Russian vaccine.

I couldn't afford completely to neglect the main expedition programs while vaccination was underway, but we were getting short of personnel. Under the control of Bhanu Bannerjee a team headed back downvalley towards Chaunrikharka—our Nepalese liaison officer, who was known by his initials, "K. C.," two senior Sherpas, and a medical orderly from the Namche checkpost. In a week of concentrated effort they vaccinated several thousand people and reported a number of deaths and many illnesses.

Phil Houghton was slowly recovering from a severe attack of glandular fever and was finding it all he could do to deal with the many people who came every day into Khumjung from the surrounding villages. Desmond Doig and I returned from a trip upvalley to discover that the smallpox had spread to Thami, a large village towards the Tibetan border. Weak though he was and unable to walk for any distance, Phil had clambered aboard the headman's pony and galloped off with a couple of Sherpas to initiate a vaccination program. Meanwhile we received representatives from both Phorche and Pangboche villages beseeching us to vaccinate their people. We promised to do all we could.

Several days later Desmond and I approached the village of Thami up the foaming Bhote River. We were met on the outskirts by a Sherpa matron of dignity and wealth who plied us with tea and chang in traditional Sherpa fashion. It wasn't until we had partaken liberally of these that she explained her problem. She was the wife of the headman of the lower village of Thami and three of her children were sick with smallpox. Would we come to her home and examine them?

Knowing we could do little, yet unable to refuse her request, we walked with her through the village to where her husband was waiting to meet us at the door of his solid and imposing house. We climbed up the stairs into the living room and, as my eye caught the rich carpets and numerous shiny ornaments, my thoughts returned to the extreme poverty of the house in Surkya where we now knew the poor young girl had died. Such vivid contrasts are not common among the Sherpas—there are rich and poor but the vast majority are of a solid middle class.

Despite the evident wealth it was a very sad household. Here the children had warm beds and clothing, but the disease had struck them down just the same. Sitting in bed, covered in drying scabs, was a thin boy of twelve—perhaps with the worst behind him. Near at hand was a girl of fourteen, terribly scarred and blinded, and close to death. In front of the fire lay a beautiful girl of eighteen, her slender hands and rich clothing showing that she was the pride and joy of her family. But on her face were the first dread signs of the disease. It seemed impossible to believe that this lovely girl in all her youth and strength would be unable to cast off the disease. But such proved to be the case. Although we did what we could, within the week the two girls were dead. Only the boy recovered.

Reports were now coming in from all directions about the spread of the disease, and we renewed our efforts to vaccinate as many people as we could. Vaccine was getting low and further supplies had not yet arrived by mail runner, as had been promised. Then I remembered the small amount of vaccine sent in long before to the American expedition and dispatched a message about it to their base camp several days' march up the valley.

Norman Dyhrenfurth, the expedition leader, responded

immediately. His doctors had already vaccinated the Sherpas employed by the expedition, but most of their vaccine was unused. He sent this to us immediately and it enabled us to keep our vaccination program in operation until ample supplies arrived a few days later by runner.

By now we had a clear picture of how the disease had come into Khumbu and how one infected individual could cause so much suffering and distress.

It all started with a Sherpa from the Khumbu region who traveled out to Katmandu looking for work as a porter with the American Everest Expedition. He obtained this job and carried a sixty-pound load over the long, hilly route into the Dudh Kosi Valley. At Chyangma he first complained to his companions of fever and upset, but carried his load with the dogged determination of his kind. At Taksindu, the monastery above the Dudh Kosi River, he showed signs of the disease—blisters on his face—and found himself unable to handle the load. His relatives and friends rallied around and split the sixty pounds between them so that he wouldn't lose a day's pay. Very sick now, he stopped for breakfast in a house in Surkya—the house where two people later died (including our girl patient). He staggered on all afternoon and spent the night at a house in the village above Chaunrikharka. Also staying in the house were a boy of twelve and a girl of fourteen from Thami (whom we were to meet later). They had been downvalley collecting food for their family and were traveling back with the American expedition for company and security. The sick man got little farther than this. He died next day in a house beside the river. All those who had been in contact with him went on to carry the infection throughout the villages of Khumbu. By the time the epidemic had run its course we had vaccinated over 7000 people, but we knew of twenty-five who had died and many more who were scarred and blinded.

To the River

In controlling the spread of the disease, we came up against some of the traditional beliefs of the Sherpas. The Sherpa custom is to cremate the dead with all religious ceremony and feasting. But for some reason—we can't find where it originated—they believe that if you cremate a person who has died of smallpox, the disease will be carried in the smoke and spread to all around. All cases of smallpox are therefore consigned to the mercies of the turbulent Himalayan rivers. My first experience of this had been many years before, in 1951, on my first visit to these same regions. In a cool, shaded valley we were crossing a mountain torrent thundering out of a steep narrow gorge. It was a hot day and we had been climbing vigorously for some time. I stopped to get a drink from the clear water and was immediately restrained by our head Sherpa, Passang Dawa Lama. "This stream is not good, sahib! Above us is the village of Lukhla, where many have died of smallpox. It is not good to burn the bodies of such people, so they have been thrown into this stream and sleep in the deep pools in that gorge up there." I have never been able to pass this wild and beautiful spot without a faint shudder at this memory and a hasty glance up into the haunted, inaccessible realms above.

Our efforts to persuade the Sherpas in ways of limiting the disease were only moderately successful. We emphasized again and again the need to burn the clothes and bedding of any victims, but this was rarely done. Clothes were too valuable and few Sherpas had the money to purchase new ones at will. After a good scrub in the local stream the garments were considered fit for their next wearer.

We expedition members were having so much contact

with smallpox victims that we started wondering about our own degree of protection. All of us had been vaccinated within the preceding twelve months, but we came from countries where the disease was more or less nonexistent, so presumably we had little natural resistance. We lined up, therefore, and Phil Houghton scratched each of us with the Russian vaccine. Alas for hopes of a modest immune reaction. The whole lot of us "took" in no uncertain fashion with fever, swollen glands and painful arms—and we were left without much confidence in our effete Western vaccinations.

The village just below Thami was one of the hardest-hit of the lot. We vaccinated everybody here except for a little pocket that held out against all our persuasions. It was a monastery of the yellow sect—the only one in the Khumbu region, where all the lamas are red-sect. Despite our pleas the head lama remained adamant. "How can we show such lack of faith in our spiritual powers?" he said. "Surely the purity of our thoughts can protect us against all ills? We are performing extra meditations and observances and, though we appreciate the kind intent of your requests, we must refuse." Despite their daily contact with infected people, none of these lamas developed smallpox, and their status in the village increased enormously. We were impressed.

In the latter stages of the smallpox epidemic we were getting requests from villages from far and wide. One of our senior Sherpas from near Junbesi, five days' march away, rushed off home when a message came saying his family were ill. He arrived to find that all were well, but stayed for a few days to vaccinate his village. In our base camp at Khumjung we were visited by a well-dressed and well-spoken young man who carried a petition from the panchyat of Jubing, a village of Nepalese and Sherpas three days' march down the river. This petition said there was much sickness in the village. They beseeched us to give the young man some vaccine. He claimed to have previous vaccination experience and, when Phil Houghton tested him out, proved to be quite competent.

I could ill afford to spare anyone for a week or more to accompany this man, so requested the checkpost captain to send his medical orderly and offered to pay for his food and porters. Some time later I received my reply from the checkpost—the medical orderly was ill and couldn't go, but the Jubing man had departed with the vaccine. It was a day or two before our Sherpas told us what they had known all along—the man was certainly from near Jubing, but he had written and signed the petition himself. He had accepted money from his neighbors on the promise that he would get vaccine for them, and get it he had. Local rumor put it that he expected to make Rs 1500 out of the deal—a tidy profit for a week or two of work.

A month or so later we had a visit in Khumjung from the commissioner of police for the whole district. A thin, shrewd ex-soldier, he was the most senior government official ever to visit this region. After dining with us and discussing the various problems of the area, he came around to the point of his visit. In the Jubing area people had told him that Hillary Sahib's men had been vaccinating people and charging a fee for it. Could I tell him the truth of the matter?

I explained how we had been thoroughly tricked by the confidence man and of our ambition to meet him again sometime. The commissioner's quiet utterances boded ill for the trickster. Next morning a policeman was dispatched downvalley to take him into custody.

For three more weeks we heard no more of the matter and the commissioner had long since returned to his headquarters in Okaldunga. Then one afternoon I noted the policeman, shabby and hungry-looking, hovering about the camp and asked that he be brought in. In rather shamefaced fashion he related his story. He had gone to Jubing as instructed to arrest the man, only to find the bird had flown.

For several weeks he had followed him from village to village without success and now he was hungry and tired and scared to return to Okaldunga and face the wrath of his commissioner. "What shall I do, sahib?"

I questioned him about the Jubing man's activities. Yes, he had taken money for his vaccination services—a total of forty-seven rupees (six dollars). He had also vaccinated a lot of other people in Jubing and not charged anything for it. As the story unfolded, my annoyance at being tricked faded away.

"Will you give me my instructions, sahib? If you wish I will rest up for a few days and then return to Jubing and beat the man until he is close to death?" This seemed rather drastic a treatment for a mere forty-seven rupees. Obviously the man had been thoroughly frightened and would think twice before trying such a trick again. I sent a much relieved policeman back to his commissioner with a note saying I felt that justice had been served.

Of all the programs we carried out on the expedition— schools, waterworks, medical clinics, and the like—the one most widely appreciated was undoubtedly the vaccination, and this hadn't been part of my original plans.

"You have saved all our lives," said the four village head-men of Khumjung when they came with chang and scarves to express their thanks. "But for you we would all now be dead. You are undoubtedly the father and mother of our village!" Looking at their tough, gnarled faces I personally doubted it—only Father Time would catch up with them. Protesting a little, we bowed our heads in acceptance of their gifts and joined with them to drink their chang long into the night.

Chapter 4

PANGBOCHE—SCHOOLHOUSE IN THE CLOUDS

Pangboche was one of the first villages to petition me for a school. It is the closest village to Everest and sprawls over a scanty terrace high above the Imja River. The people are mostly poorer than in the neighboring villages, and they have locally the reputation of being unreliable and dishonest. But on several expeditions I have known a number of the better Pangboche Sherpas, and they have proved just as hardy and loyal as the rest of them. Life in Pangboche is even more rigorous than in the ordinary Sherpa village, and perhaps this has made the people more suspicious and less demonstrative. No words of praise have been written by expeditions about Pangboche—only complaints about the pilfering, and hard words about the local insistence on being paid for everything and paid in more than full. This seemed a place that badly needed a school.

On April 1 Desmond Doig, Murray Ellis and I left Khumjung, bound for Pangboche. In heavily falling snow we strolled along the spectacular rocky path above the Dudh Kosi River and then plunged down the abrupt two thousand feet to the river itself. Above us the long, rising track clung to the side of the steep spur leading to the Monastery of Thyangboche; we puffed our way up this slope, which never seems to get any shorter or any easier. We reached the crest in fast fading light. Through the whirling snow we could see tall, distinguished figures waiting for us at the ornately decorated entrance arch of the monastery grounds. It was the head lama himself, some of his senior lamas, and old friend Dawa Tenzing, veteran of a score of tough expeditions.

Doing us much honor, the head lama led us across the grassy crest of the spur to the new monastery rest house. Largely donated to the monastery by Dawa Tenzing, this rest house filled an urgent need in supplying accommodation for distinguished visitors—religious dignitaries, village headmen and expedition members. Much of the timber had been salvaged from the "Green Hut" my expedition had built at 17,000 feet in the Mingbo Valley some two and a half years before, and it was satisfying to see it being put to such good use. The head lama showed us around with great pride and then beckoned us over to a table spread with food. We sat down in jovial mood and had placed before us delicate china cups resting on exquisitely carved silver-and-gold stands. After drinking ceremonial tea, the head lama gave a few formal words of welcome and then departed, having invited us to dinner on the following day.

We awoke to a brilliant morning. The monastery, the trees, the peaks around, were all dressed in a layer of new snow, sparkling and gleaming in the early sun. At the head of the valley, only ten miles away, the summit of Everest, crowned with a long plume of wind-blown snow, thrust up into the blue Tibetan sky. Our walk up the valley to Pangboche was a delight. The landscape was incredibly beautiful under its new snow and reinforced my belief that this is surely one of the loveliest places on the surface of the earth. Even Pangboche itself looked clean and peaceful.

Our first visit was to the gompa, where we paid our respects to the lamas and laid an offering of Rs 100 ($13) on the altar. Slowly the village elders gathered while I waited with an outward show of patience I certainly didn't feel. When a quorum was present we moved off leisurely up rapidly drying paths to the ridge above the village. Here on a piece of communal land the village had chosen the

site for the school, and nearby was a huge pile of rocks
gathered for the school building.

In Pangboche flat land is at a premium and I had no
desire to use the best arable land, which is urgently needed
for food. But this site had many limitations. A building
could be constructed on it but there was no room for a
playground, and my eyes kept straying to the dry wash
funneling down from the slopes above. I strolled over to a
group of rocks piled in the form of an open fireplace and
noticed ashes and half-burned remnants of many fires.

"What is this fireplace doing out here?" I queried.

"It is the burning ghat for cremating the dead," was the
reply, "and it will be necessary for the lamas to have many
prayers and ceremonies before it can be moved elsewhere."
The thought of the delays and expense of such a proceeding
was rather daunting, and we all sat around in the sun in a
glum silence.

Finally someone made a suggestion. Farther up the ridge
was an old house for sale—the house wasn't very good and
the land was very poor so the total price was only Rs 600
($80). Were we interested? We were. Anything was better
than the religious problem of moving a burning ghat. En
masse we drifted up the hill, surmounted a little crest and
then came suddenly on an old rock house surrounded by
two small potato fields enclosed in dry-rock walls. We
stopped, enchanted. It was the most glorious position. A
hundred feet below us the gompa and houses of Pangboche
lay spread-eagled in the warm sun. On every side were
tremendous mountain vistas—Everest to the north, Ama
Dablam and Kangtega to the east, Numbur to the south
and Taweche directly above to the west.

Protected by a rock wall from the sharp wind, we sat in
the sun and discussed the matter. After careful deliberation
the headman agreed that the village would try to raise the
money for the land by levying a charge on each house—
"but we must have time, sahib." This was a worthy sugges-

tion but time was now more important to us than money. Desmond, Murray and I had our own little conference. Murray felt we should start clearing operations on the site immediately, and Desmond and I agreed. I put to the village another proposition. I would purchase the land and donate it to the village for the school. The village in return must reaffirm its intention of giving free labor for the clearing of the land, the assembling of rocks, and the carrying of timber from the forest. The foresters, carpenters and stonemasons would be employed by us. The elders accepted this offer with enthusiasm and assured us that villagers would start demolition work on the site next day. We agreed that the necessary documents would be drawn up and brought to Thyangboche in the morning for signing in the presence of the head lama. Everything had gone amazingly well and we were in high spirits as we strode back down the valley to Thyangboche.

"Tea"

At 5 P.M. we went to the monastery to have tea with the head lama. First we made our bows in the great temple and I placed an offering on the altar. Then we were conducted by a young lama along a narrow alley and through a heavy door into a paved courtyard. Here we were greeted by a ferocious Tibetan mastiff, who threw himself against his chain in frantic efforts to get at us. The young lama took hold of the brute's collar and pulled him back out of the way, but we were glad to slip past the snapping jaws onto dark, winding stairs and up into the head lama's private room. This was small but beautifully decorated, and the window framed the most stupendous view of Kangtega. Sitting cross-legged on a carpeted bench in the window alcove was the head lama, dressed in gorgeous brocades. We each in turn presented him with scarves and presents and received his blessing. For the next hour we sipped Tibetan tea—a horrifying mixture of black tea, salt and rancid yak butter. The head lama was in fine form and most vivacious. He and Desmond and I were old friends, so formalities went by the board. The Nepali interchange of gossip became too quick for me to hope to follow.

Finally food appeared. First a greasy soup made from venerable yak—and with the full flavor that only year-old meat can give. Despite my long experience of this dish I had difficulty in getting it down, but my discomfort was relieved a little by observing the suffering of Murray Ellis, a conservative New Zealand eater, tackling his first traditional Tibetan meal. Next course was rice, fried yak, fried potato chips and a thicker soup from the same old yak. We all managed to do better with this. Dessert was a large bowl of dahi (curds) with sugar added, and we devoured this with enthusiasm. Yak dahi is excellent food, and with the addition of sugar and tsampa (cooked ground barley) is popular with all expeditions.

The head lama's room had no heating, and a vigorous breeze came through the partly open window. Outside I could see Kangtega outlined against the cold night sky; there were signs of a hard frost. Sitting on a cushion in the unaccustomed cross-legged position, I was rapidly becoming stiff with cold despite my down jacket. But the lightly clad lama seemed unaffected by the temperature and chatted gaily on. At 7:30 P.M. I'd had all I could stand and politely suggested that we had taken too much of the lama's time and must now leave him in peace. But no, he said, we must have our final ceremonial cup of tea. Fortunately someone took pity on us and the tea was hot and sweetened, the milk fresh. We left the head lama with mutual expressions of affection and esteem and scurried across the frosty sward to our warm sleeping bags in the rest house.

It was with reluctance that we crawled out of bed next morning, for it was cold although the sun was shining on the peaks above. We were immediately advised that we had been commanded to breakfast with the abbot of Thyangboche—the second in seniority in the monastery. A combined groan went up from the three of us. Dried, matured yak is hard enough to take in the evening—but for *breakfast?* No, we couldn't do it! Despite our obvious distress Sirdar Mingmatsering was adamant—go we must or insult our hosts. We staggered outside and watched clouds writhing around the summit of Everest. Then we marched off to the execution. The abbot is a wonderfully genial old man whom I remembered from as far back as 1951. He welcomed us with glasses of raw rakshi. Then breakfast was placed before us. It was as bad as we had feared—Tibetan tea with rice and yak stew. The day was saved by the final dish— hot fresh yak's milk with tsampa and sugar—and this helped quiet our queasy stomachs.

At the appointed time we gathered at the rest house for the meeting with the Pangboche villagers and the signing of documents, and were there joined by the head lama attended by two of his junior lamas. After an hour's delay the only people who had turned up from Pangboche were the old mother of the owner (who himself lived in Katmandu) and the man who was acting as agent for the land —no headman, no elders, no Pangboche lamas. It was becoming clear that things had gone far too easily the previous day—the village had taken it all as a game not to be played too seriously.

"How is work going on the school site?"

"No one turned up."

"Where is everyone?"

"Digging their potato fields and upvalley, grazing their yaks."

The head lama advised us not to complete the deal for the land. It was agreed that Dawa Tenzing and the head lama's secretary would go to Pangboche the next day and find out definitely whether a school was wanted or not. A

diary entry illustrates my feelings at the time. "Pangboche
is so backward in every way that it badly needs a school.
But there seems some doubt in our Sherpas' minds whether
the parents will take their children away from work and
send them to school. In general the village is terribly poor
and the inhabitants notoriously moronic. Would it be better
to transfer the school to the smaller village of Phorche, where
the people are a more cheerful and robust type?"

"You must be patient with Pangboche," said the head
lama. "My people at times behave like children and must
be treated as such. You must be patient!" Dawa Tenzing
drew us into his house as we departed and thrust into our
hands large bowls of excellent chang. "Drink it," he said;
"it will be a horse for your road." Ten minutes later we
were striding through a heavy snowstorm on our way back
to Khumjung.

We didn't have long to wait for a reply from Pangboche.
Next day it was still snowing when a group of men appeared, led by the head lama's secretary. It was all a mistake, they explained. They hadn't realized there was a meeting at Thyangboche. Already thirty-five children were
signed up and these would definitely not go up to the Ding-
boche fields for the potato planting. As soon as the word was
given they'd dash madly down to Khumjung and carry the
building material back up to Pangboche. Finally, they'd already started to demolish the old house. I was a little
skeptical of this enthusiasm but the head lama's secretary
assured me there had been a misunderstanding and recom-
mended we go ahead with the deal. I paid over the Rs 600
and we received the signed documents. Then I asked
Dawa Tenzing to represent our interests in Pangboche and
the villagers promised to give him every support in prepar-
ing the site for the school.

By April 10 we were ready to move to Pangboche and
start our construction program. The majority of the party
carried the building equipment over the shorter route via

Thyangboche and vaccinated everyone as they went. Desmond, Murray and I went the long way around via the village of Phorche, for we wanted to meet the panchyat and assess the interest and enthusiasm of the village for a school in the future. The route to Phorche is a spectacular one. The track climbs through the vast rock bluffs above Khumjung on wooden staircases and delicately perched rock platforms. Then you plunge steeply down into a narrow gorge enclosing the Dudh Kosi River. With knees quivering from the solid pounding of your descent, you cross the cantilever bridge and then climb steeply up the other side through twisted rhododendrons draped with long fingers of silver moss. Cupped in a smiling hollow on the flanks of Tawcche, Phorche has a charm all its own. Mountains are all around, but you are hardly conscious of them. The village lies in the warm sun and your eyes instinctively follow the river to the south, over the foothills of Nepal towards the throbbing plains of India. Phorche has no easy approach— it is frequently cut off even from the other Sherpa villages —and yet its warmth and aspect make you forget at times that you are living high on a grim Himalayan peak.

There are fifty to sixty houses in the village, and we seemed to visit most of them to be plied with chang, rakshi and hospitality. The elders conducted us to the site they had chosen for a school—a gorgeous position amongst spidery trees on the edge of a huge bluff—but one careless kick of a ball and its next stop would be 2000 feet down in the Dudh Kosi River. I told the village elders they should plan to send their children to Pangboche School for the next few years and we would then try and get them a school of their own. But the elders shook their heads. "It is too far for our children to go to Pangboche each day, sahib, and the track is too narrow and dangerous."

In a haze of bonhomie, we carried on to Pangboche, following the tiny twisting track high above the valley floor. Slips and bluffs, loose traverses and falling rocks made it an adventurous trip and we could easily understand the reluctance of Phorche to send their children over it. But the villagers' enthusiasm for education had been so encouraging that I was determined to think up some way of helping them.

Camp at Pangboche was set up on a terrace above the village in a pleasant grove of stunted pine trees. A tinkling stream was near at hand and there was a tremendous sweep of valley and mountains in front of the tent doors. I wasted no time in camp—I wanted to see what progress had been made on the school site and rumor had it that the village had been slothful and disinterested. I climbed up to the ridge to find women and children swarming over the place like ants, carrying rocks and timber and leveling out the rough spots (as I found later, there had been a sudden increase of workers on the day of our arrival). Progress had not been as rapid as we had hoped but at least *some* progress had been made.

Dawa Tenzing, the masons and carpenters, Murray Ellis, Desmond and I gathered on the site to lay out the foundations of the school building. The back and side walls were to be of rock and would be constructed by the Sherpa masons.

"How many inches wide are the rock walls, Dawa Tenzing?" we asked.

"Inches, sahib? We don't measure in inches. The width of the wall is the distance from the mason's elbow to the tips of his fingers."

With a broad grin the chief mason presented his arm for measurement—about eighteen inches more or less. Under Murray's watchful eye we laid out the positions for the walls and took the necessary levels. Then we were brushed aside as the masons rolled big rocks into position for the cornerstones. It soon became apparent that Dawa Tenzing and the masons regarded us as hindrances when rock walls were being built, so we slunk off to camp. Later in the afternoon I returned unannounced to the school site to inspect progress on the foundations. To Dawa Tenzing's chagrin I arrived just at the wrong moment—they had discovered that one of their walls was ten inches out of line and were laboriously shifting the stones. I refrained from comment but resolved that a quiet check on distances and angles wouldn't be a bad idea.

The weather in Khumbu had been unstable for some time and as the Pangboche School was at 13,500 feet, we were getting daily falls of snow—rarely more than a couple of inches but enough to make work on the building a cold and arduous business. For the next week I left Bhanu Bannerjee in charge at Pangboche with instructions to harry the masons unmercifully and get the rock walls finished as soon as possible.

Over small radio transceivers we kept in touch with Bhanu and he told us of his many problems. One morning he reported 3 inches of fresh snow and a dense fog; another time it was shortage of labor to carry rocks; then one day nobody turned up. Religious festival.

On April 21 we moved back to Pangboche in force with the intention of getting on with the main building program. I found all sorts of troubles in the village. The stonemasons and carpenters were doing a good job but they were constantly hampered by lack of labor to collect stones, as had been promised. Little of the timber had been carried from the forests, and worst of all, none of the children had turned up for enrollment at the announced time. About the enrollment we received a variety of comments:

"They'll be enrolled in seven days."

"The lamas have to give their blessings."

"They're too busy digging the potato fields at the moment."

I summoned the headmen to a meeting on the school site. After much delay they all appeared. This time there was a new addition—the senior headman, who had been away previously on a trading trip.

He was a much more sophisticated character than his compatriots and seemed determined to be obstructive. Why hadn't the village supplied the labor they had promised? we asked. It was all our fault, the headman advised. We had vaccinated the village for smallpox and as a result everyone had been prostrate and unable to work. We pointed out that Khumjung and Thami had also been vaccinated but they had still managed to turn out in force. But he only scowled and muttered about "when the village was good and ready!"

In a fine old fury I gave an ultimatum—tomorrow there'd be a man from each house carrying timber and the children would all enroll or we'd pick up our building material and put a school at Phorche instead. I stamped off, leaving them in a stunned silence, and Desmond, Tom and Phil only waited to deliver a few more well-chosen words before departing as well.

As we sat around camp, sipping tea and simmering over the injustices of the world, another crisis was rapidly developing.

Horror Story

One of our young Sherpas, Purbu Chundu, was a favorite nephew of the famous sirdar, Passang Dawa Lama. He now appeared before us in the grip of fierce emotion and asked permission to tell his story.

He explained that in 1962 he had been a member of a German expedition of which his uncle was sirdar. This expedition had tackled the formidable peak, Pumori, a mountain which had rebuffed a number of previous expeditions. The German party was not to be denied and they forced a difficult and spectacular route to the summit. On the descent of the mountain the assault team was very late and

16. A first-timer to the Himalayas, Dr. Phillip Houghton is shown with head lama of Thyangboche

17. Murray Ellis proves himself a very practical engineer

18. Desmond Doig — linguist, artist, humanitarian — keeps life from being mundane

19. Sir Edmund and Lady Hillary among honored spectators at the Khum-jung School Sports Day

20. Jim Wilson, a minister with a
lengthening record of difficult climbs

21. Tom Frost: for a twenty-minute interview he drove 1660 miles

22. Mike Gill's important Ama Dablam climb and Dave Dornan's excellent
experience in Alaska were to serve them well

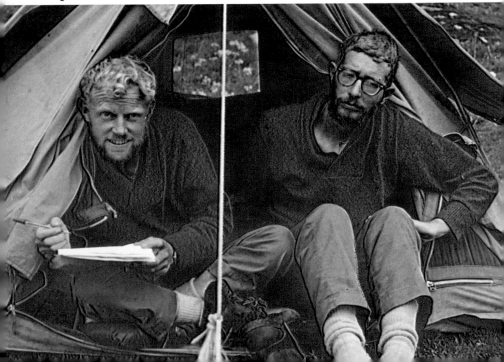

the weather had become cold and thick. On one rope were
two men, the only Swiss climber in the party and an experienced Sherpa. Tired from their climb and baffled by the
bad visibility, the two men strayed too close to the edge of
a bluff and when the snow underneath gave way they
plunged thousands of feet to their deaths.

On the other rope were three men—two Germans and the
renowned Sherpa, Annullu, who had first made his name
with us on Everest in 1953. Only after a terrible struggle
were these men able to make their escape. At one stage the
two Germans slid off in an avalanche and only a superhu-
man effort by Annullu was able to prevent them all from
being swept away. The cold powder snow and the bitter
weather took their toll and the men's extremities were
white and frostbitten before they reached safety in their assault camp.

Purbu explained how next day they had started the
search for the bodies of the two men and had found them
on the glacier at the foot of the mountain. Two graves were
made for the men in a deep crevasse. The expedition leader
placed in the Sherpa's grave his down jacket as a bed and
in the grave of the Swiss his colorful wool sweater. Then the
bodies were lowered gently into place and after a short
ceremony rocks were piled high above them. Over the Swiss
a cross was erected and over the Sherpa a Buddhist chorten.

Quite a number of high-altitude Sherpas and ordinary
porters were present at the funeral, said Purbu, including a
man from Pangboche—the village elder we called the Nike,
who was now helping build the school. Purbu quickly came
to the heart of the matter. Yesterday he had seen the Nike
wearing a jersey that was far too big for him. "Even the
sahibs noticed the jersey and made jokes about it," said
Purbu. He had recognized it as the jersey from the grave.

I sent Mingmatsering to see if he could get the Nike to
come to our camp, but he proved hard to find. It wasn't un-

til we were crowded around the campfire after tea that he was led up to us. Desmond started to question him quietly.

"Yes," he admitted quite freely, "I was wearing the pullover that belonged to the dead sahib."

After further prompting he conceded that he also had the down jacket belonging to the Sherpa.

"How did you get them?" asked Desmond. The response was glib and well prepared. "I was given them by Sirdar Passang Dawa Lama."

At this accusation against his uncle, Purbu Chundu sprang to his feet and with eyes full of fire asserted that this was an outright lie. "I was with my uncle all the time after the accident," he said, "and at no time did he go near the graves. In fact he warned everyone (including the Nike) that if the graves were disturbed he would come back and kill them with his own hands. Already in Darjeeling the wife of the dead Sherpa has heard rumors that a man has been seen in Pangboche wearing the ring she had given her husband on their wedding day!"

At this fierce denunciation the Nike hastily withdrew his story and replaced it with another. Some time after the accident, he said, he happened to be strolling up on this lonely glacier and he'd come upon the opened graves. To his astonishment he'd found the pullover and down jacket stuffed carelessly under a rock. They were too good to waste and he'd brought them home.

I had been listening to this tale with growing horror. The man was so obviously lying and was so confident that nothing could be done about it anyway that my gorge rose. When he cracked a hearty joke with the silent ring of Sherpas round about I could stand it no longer. I leaped up and thumped him vigorously around the ears and knocked him down. He scrambled about on his hands and knees, trying to escape, and presented the seat of his pants to my irate gaze. Next moment I had delivered a mighty kick to send him tumbling down the hill into the darkness.

Whether it was my ultimatum to the village or harsh treatment of the Nike I don't know, but early next morning we heard signs of action in the village and saw loads of timber starting to come up the long climb from the river. At breakfast time the headman and Dawa Tenzing arrived in conciliatory vein and assured us that all the timber would be brought up by the end of the day.

At 10 A.M. we gathered on the school site for the enrollment of children. Nobody had yet appeared but first one little family group and then another—all spick and span in their best clothes—left their homes and climbed slowly up towards us. Everyone gathered around as teacher Tem Dorje took particulars and then instructed the parents to sign the register with their thumb marks. Each parent had to agree to leave his children at the school at all times and not take them away for yak tending or potato planting. By the end of the day we had thirty-five children enrolled. I had been surprised at their caliber. I suppose I had expected a group of morons but this red-cheeked and sparkling-eyed group didn't look much different from any group of children anywhere.

Half a day's walk up the valley from us was the encampment of a small German scientific expedition. I had sent them a message about the Nike's activities and two of them arrived the same afternoon. They considered it their duty to visit the sites of the graves and re-establish them if necessary. I agreed to make Purbu Chundu available for this. When weather permitted, the Germans trekked up to the foot of Pumori. The mountain had done the job for them. A huge avalanche had swept down over the graves, covering everything in millions of tons of ice and leaving the dead men to sleep peacefully and undisturbed.

Desmond and I were determined that the Nike should be punished by the authorities for his crime. Our liaison officer, "K. C.," had authority to represent the government and marched off to place the Nike under arrest. He found him lying in bed, groaning and holding onto his head and claiming he was about to die—whether from shame or from my blows wasn't quite clear. K. C. warned him not to try to escape and placed a guard outside his door.

By now my wrath had subsided considerably and, although I still regarded the Nike as a nasty piece of work, I couldn't help feeling that in a way he was a product of his village. The other headmen were now freely admitting that they'd known about the Nike's activities all along and though they hadn't approved of his actions, they'd never raised their voices in censure in the village council. This attitude is common indeed amongst the Sherpas and is a direct consequence of their religious beliefs. They accept the existence of cause and effect and are all too ready to explain away any misdeed by saying that it wouldn't have happened to the victim if his karma hadn't attracted it to him. The Sherpas will rarely combine together against a bully or even put in a complaint to the police. They prefer to accept the bully and criminal as an ordinary member of society who will receive his punishment in due course—but they don't want to be the ones giving the punishment, as by so doing their soul may be linked by cause and effect with that of the transgressor for many reincarnations. Perhaps this basic trait is at the back of many of their more charming qualities as well, but when an emergency arises one can't help wishing for a little more materialism.

When K. C. and the senior headman suggested that the Nike should not be handed over to the police but should be subjected to the village "disgracing" ceremony, I was only too happy to agree. The Nike had been given a considerable scare and his disgrace in front of his neighbors would serve as a salutary lesson to the village.

In the middle of the afternoon we gathered in the courtyard of the gompa and a miserable Nike was brought stumbling in with a bandage around his head, completely crushed by the whole proceeding. He seated himself in the gloom of a corner with his head between his hands. Desmond refused to allow this—the man must face his punishment in the open—and he instructed the headman to have the Nike brought out in front of the people. He sat on the bottom step of the gompa with a weeping sister on one side and his stalwart and dry-eyed wife on the other.

The tension built up to a high pitch as the proceedings commenced. First a document was read to the assembled gathering, a confession from the Nike in which he admitted his guilt but pleaded for mercy and forgiveness. Then another, longer document, signed by all the senior men of the village, in which they condemned the Nike's action and guaranteed that such a thing would not happen in the village again. I was then called on to say a few words to be translated into Nepali by Desmond, and into Sherpa by Mingmatsering. By now I was feeling rather sorry for the Nike, who must have been undergoing mental torture, and my words were brief: a suggestion that he had been punished in the sight of his equals and it was now up to him to rehabilitate himself by his actions over the next few years. Desmond, too, had few words to say but they were telling ones.

"We can forgive your crime," he declaimed to the crouching man. "But you will have to make your own peace with God!"

There was a deathly hush after this statement, broken only by the sobs of the Nike's sister, and there was no doubt that these last words had made a strong impression.

The Nike and his family were asked if they had anything to say, but the man was glad to be silent. Only his wife, a tall, handsome woman, wanted to speak. Still dry-eyed, with a hard set to her jaw, she repeated the story of the discovery of the clothes—how her husband had found them under a rock. When questioned by the headman, she admitted that this was the story her husband had told her. The headman shrugged his shoulders and passed on.

We admired the way this woman had supported her husband, although there seemed little emotion in her reactions. Later we discovered that her background had given her some training in such crises: she was a "fallen" nun, a category accepted but not really approved by this non-critical Buddhist community. And her brother was the biggest racketeer and strong-arm man in the Khumbu area.

I was glad when the proceedings were over and we could see the shattered Nike being led off to his house. Undoubtedly this function had been good for the village. Not only the Nike had been under judgment. We knew that in a week's time the Nike would be drinking chang with his fellows as though nothing had happened, but suspected that the village might still remember the original cause.

A few days later the Nike's wife made a pilgrimage to Thyangboche. Her husband had been sorely shaken by Desmond's comment on making his peace with God, and she was bearing gifts and a request that the head lama intercede. Three times she saw the head lama and stated her husband's plea and three times she was turned away. "This man has committed a great crime," said the head lama. "He must work out his own salvation."

Skylight to the Clouds

Our firm stand in the village had produced immediate improvement in the support we received for the school construction, and real progress was made over the next few days. The daily bad weather was making climbing conditions on the mountains both difficult and dangerous, and I recalled a reluctant group off Taweche to come and help us with the building program. The school site had become a hive of industry. In one corner two men with an 8-foot saw were pitsawing balks of timber into rafters, beams and planks; the masons were putting the final touches to the rock walls; the carpenters were completing the joinery for the windows and the decorative frieze, called *langdy pangdy,* which was to come under the overhanging roof; the school children were gathering rocks for the enclosing walls of the playground; most of the sahibs were sawing and hammering at the floor and framework; and Desmond Doig was building a seesaw and swing. Already the building was taking shape and our pride in it was growing accordingly.

The weather was still harassing us. Fresh snow on the rafters made them slippery and dangerous and a stiff wind whistled around our ears, making down clothing a necessity. During the worst spells we'd come off the building and crowd around a blazing fire with our umbrellas up and the snow weighing them down. In the few moments when the clouds lifted we could see the mountains heavily plastered with snow, and sounds of frequent avalanches rumbled across the valley.

"This is the worst winter we have known for a generation," said the Sherpas, "and still the summer refuses to come. When can we plant the rest of our potatoes?"

Under our determined onslaught the building grew rapidly. The floor joists were placed in position and the flooring timbers securely nailed down. The heavy central beam was raised with much grunting and groaning, and the rafters were cut and then hammered into position. To combat the vigorous winds that could be expected here, we threaded wires through the rock walls a foot from the top and nailed these securely onto the roof structure. It was quite an exciting moment when we were ready to put the corrugated aluminum onto the roof. Dave Dornan and I started this and made haste with such enthusiasm that we didn't notice we were lining up the sheets a little out of plumb. Perfectionist Murray Ellis came to supervise our work and to our chagrin made us pull off a dozen sheets and put them back square. Despite such setbacks we completed the covering of the roof in a day. Our particular pride was the sheets of corrugated Fiberglas we had set into the roof as skylights. It was already apparent how effective they were going to be.

To our delight, the next two days were fine. The snow rapidly disappeared from the ground around us and black rock could be seen again on the peaks above. We reveled in the warm sun and hurried on to the last jobs, perhaps the most difficult ones—the fitting of windows into the front and side walls, the hanging of the door, and the cutting and nailing of planking onto the front wall. These would not have been problems with square-cut timber, but with the irregular product of pitsawing it was difficult to produce a good flush finish. There were many grumbles and complaints before all the holes were blocked and our sliding aluminum-frame windows from Chicago were safely in place and causing gasps of admiration from the local experts.

Desmond and I were still worrying about how to arrange schooling for the children of Phorche. The only solution to their isolation seemed for them to stay in Pangboche for the week and return home on weekends. On investigation we found that it would be prohibitively expensive for the children to be boarded out with individual families. The practical answer was to have them all living together. After much negotiation we managed to lease one of the biggest and newest houses in the village. The rent was Rs 200 ($27) per annum, so I signed the lease for three years and paid the money in advance. The lease was then presented to the village of Phorche. We worked on the house, transforming one end of the upper story into a comfortable room for Mr. Phutenzi, the schoolteacher. The elders of Phorche came in force to examine the house and were happy with it. They advised us that seventeen of their children were coming to the Pangboche School. Various adults would take turns living in the house to maintain discipline.

Opening day for the school was April 29. It was a patchy

morning with sun at first, but by midday we were enveloped in a warm drizzle. We had hoped for brilliant sunshine. Our Sherpas were far from despondent. "This weather is most propitious, sahib," they said. "We need the warm rain for our potatoes. The gods must be looking with high favor on our new school."

At 12:30 the head lama of Thyangboche entered the village, and at 1 P.M. approached the school with a long procession. Despite the rain it was a colorful and cheerful scene. People had come from far and near. All the Pangboche children and parents were there in their best finery —even the Nike with his pretty daughter—and there was a strong contingent from Phorche. As a special treat for this occasion, we had brought eighteen bright-faced children from the Khumjung School. We crowded into the new school for the ceremony, with the patter of rain on the roof adding to the din of cheerful voices. The many who couldn't get inside crowded at the windows, oblivious of the rain, and we were afraid that the walls would burst under the pressure. But the speeches, the exchanging of scarves, the ceremonial drinks, the blessings by the head lama all went off without hitch in an atmosphere of warmth and goodwill.

After the ceremony we had Tibetan dancing by the people of Pangboche and, as a crowning event, a series of songs by the Khumjung school children. Their Nepalese songs were quite delightful but we had to hide our smiles a little when we heard English nursery rhymes rendered with vim, vigor and very little accuracy.

The Pangboche School started with a roll of fifty-four pupils, ranging in age from five years to twenty-six. Two of the men in the village were determined to learn to read and write and had signed themselves on as pupils at the same time they had enrolled their little daughters of six and seven. For the two months the school was in operation before I left the area they attended classes regularly. As all the pupils were starting completely from scratch irrespective of age, I asked Phutenzi how the progress of the fathers was comparing with that of their little daughters. "There is no comparison, sahib. The daughters are already far in advance of their parents. Their little minds remember things so much more easily."

It is our hope that the school in Pangboche will transform it. No longer will the village be regarded as a den of thieves by Sherpa and expedition alike. We are confident that the basic material is the same as in any village, and by education and guidance it can learn to follow more closely the pattern of cheerful tolerance and natural dignity which is so much a part of the Sherpas we love. And we have learned, too, from Pangboche—learned not to judge a village by the grubbiness of its faces or the poverty of its homes. Where opportunity has been completely lacking, how can we expect people to meet standards we accept as routine—but too often flout ourselves? We are expecting much from Pangboche's schoolhouse in the clouds!

Chapter 5

"MAYBE SHE'LL GO, MAYBE SHE WON'T"

TAWECHE, 21,463 feet, is one of the group of spectacular peaks which flank the approaches to Everest. Difficult but accessible, it offers an ideal climbing objective for an expedition, but in the past it had been neglected as being too small for a major expedition, yet too difficult to be treated as a secondary objective. In 1960 I had spent some time examining the mountain with binoculars from the Mingbo Valley and became convinced that a possible route existed somewhere up the giant couloir which cleaves the northeast face of the mountain. I asked Peter Mulgrew to do a reconnaissance of this area and he took with him several experienced Sherpas. From a lake at 17,000 feet he ascended—"by easy scrambling," he reported—to a small ice field at just over 18,000 feet. He decided that my route up the couloir was quite impracticable, but in his view there was a possible route up another clearly defined couloir to the crest of the southeast ridge. He had no time to pursue his investigations further and had to withdraw, but "Peter's Couloir" became our main hope for a chink in the armor of Taweche's defenses.

Our view of Taweche from above Khumjung had produced universal agreement that the long and spiky northwest ridge was perhaps too formidable a barrier. The south ridge, almost indistinguishable in its drop towards us, didn't hold out much promise, and only on the large buttress of the southeast ridge did we see much hope of getting a foothold. The track to Pangboche gave us a clear view of the upper section of the south ridge and confirmed our feelings that there was little there to attract us. It left us then with the two alternatives, the southeast ridge or "Peter's Couloir" on the northeast face. Either of these routes would bring the party out onto the snow plateau which undergirds the steep slopes of the summit pyramid at nearly 20,000 feet. Here, we felt, an assault camp could be safely established, leaving only about 1500 feet to be climbed on the final day. Obviously the summit pyramid was formidably steep; but whatever our disagreements on the best route to the plateau, or the possibility of reaching it at all, we generally felt confident that once camp was established there, the peak would be ours.

No one spent more time on Taweche or put more effort into the mountain than Jim Wilson, so I will leave it to him to tell the story of the assault.

Taweche
(BY JIM WILSON)

In the gompa of Pangboche village, the painted mask which does duty as a representation of the village's god Taweche is appropriately ferocious. On the morning of April 10, 1963, Dave Dornan and I stood with other expedition members watching a ceremony of propitiation to this awesome figure; we could perhaps be forgiven if we noted with alarm that not all the muttered prayers and scattered rice, nor yet our gifts of money with which the occasion climaxed, seemed to soften the grim countenance before us. For Dave and I were about to form an advance party to tackle not this mask of paper and paint, but the peak of rock and ice for which it stood. Fearsome though the mask is, the reality behind it is worse.

We went up to have a closer look at the mountain the day after we arrived at Pangboche. Ed, Murray, Dave and I reached the lake at 17,000 feet about 1 P.M. It was the highest Murray and I had been, and Ed, despite repeated references to advancing age, led the way up at a pace that I for one, found trying at that altitude. The lake was frozen solid and a bitter wind was sweeping mist over its smooth surface. It was too barren a spot to be pleasant, but it offered a good site for a base camp if the route above it should prove feasible. Through the writhing mist we had a good view of "Peter's Couloir," for the broad northeast face reared ominously above us. We had also seen from various angles on the way up the "buttress" or direct route on the southeast ridge, and we were a quiet and thoughtful group as we descended to Pangboche with the salient features of both approaches well in mind.

Mike Gill, meanwhile, had headed across the valley to his old haunts in the Mingbo. (The valley where the two high huts of the 1960–61 expedition were situated.) He argued that we were bound to be misled by the foreshortened view we would get from close under the mountain, and he was determined to get a general view from afar to compensate. Nor had he changed his mind when we thrashed matters out that night. None of the lake party had much liked Peter's route. Still under considerable snow, the face seemed a mess of steep rock and loose gullies, with outward-sloping holds half hidden by the snow. The thought of establishing a route and relaying loads on that face, with every new snowfall threatening to cut off the route or dislodge the climbers on it, failed to appeal. Moreover we had not spotted Peter's "easy scrambling" route to the ice field on the face, and access to it had seemed decidedly dubious. Hence the clean-cut lines of the buttress route, with its snow-free rock, had by contrast exercised considerable appeal, and we had perhaps softened by wishful thinking the steepness of its angle. We were for trying the buttress route first.

This suggestion provoked only scornful laughter from

Mike. "From across the valley," he insisted—and he had Polaroid photos to support his viewpoint—"you can see the true angle of that buttress. You haven't a show of getting up, let alone of taking loads up." Nettled, we invoked in return vivid pictures of the difficulties and dangers of the northeast face. The wonder of it is that we didn't abandon the whole assault forthwith, as in the argument we piled extravagance on extravagance and impossibility on top of impossibility.

Up

And now the ceremony in Pangboche Gompa was over. Its modest aim was not, we learned to our regret, to guarantee a successful ascent, nor even to provide good weather and crisp conditions. The simple but impressive propitiation was solely to ensure that we all returned safely from the mountain.

Dave is by no means cursed with the loquaciousness of his companion, but I had little doubt that his thoughts and mine were similar as we plodded up the ill-defined track above Pangboche. Can anyone set off for his first brush with a Himalayan peak and not have the same tremulous alternation between thrill and fear? It is every mountaineer's dream to climb in the Himalayas, but as the dream becomes reality, a fear lurks uneasily behind it. "What if high altitude and the responsibility of laden Sherpas test me and find me wanting?" Thus joy and uncertainty vied in my mind until the effort of moving uphill at altitude pushed all idle speculation into the background.

We were not ascending immediately to the lake. Ed had advised us to acclimatize by spending the first few nights at 16,000 feet, where a couple of stone huts and some rough walls marked a high yak pasture. The yak herds had not as yet moved up so high, and we could appropriate one of the shelters as a temporary, and comfortable, base camp. News travels though. Not long after our occupancy began, a small boy arrived and declared himself the owner's representative.

"I want rent," he announced.

Protracted negotiations hardly seemed necessary when we discovered that for the sum of one Nepalese rupee (about fourteen cents) he was happy to give us indefinite use of the hut. As in all yak-pasture shelters, a low seat was necessary to avoid smoke swirling round the ceiling, but it was pleasant, in the clean cold of a high evening, to eat companionably round the cooking fire before retreating to our tent for the night.

Our Sherpas, wise men, declined to retreat anywhere and slept round the fire. With Mingmatsering, the expedition sirdar, too valuable in the building program to be spared, Angtemba was our mountain sirdar. Eleven years of climbing experience had seen him on such peaks as Kanchenjunga (where he won his Tiger's badge for exceptional climbing achievement), Everest, Makalu, and Ama Dablam; he is a tough mountain man whose sound technique and judgment are allied with a wicked wit. Second only to him in value was the irrepressible Pembertarkay—younger, less experienced, but a natural climber and a tower of strength. Then there was Phudorje, whose brown face and never failing smile reminded us New Zealanders of cheerful Maoris at home; and Pangboche Tenzing, quieter, a very competent climber. Siku, chubby Hakpanurbu, and Karmatila made up the group for this initial probe, and we were to realize their worth many times over in the days ahead. While Dave and I had rested at Pangboche the previous day they had organized the carrying of food and equipment, and their broad grins glowed through the smoke and darkness of the hut that evening. It was comforting to know that what we lacked in local experience was amply compensated for by these cheerful companions.

Next day Angtemba, Siku, Dave and I set off to see what
the buttress approach had to offer. It was a wearisome
thousand feet to the lake, but beyond that we were on new
ground and our interest quickened. We clambered around
a subsidiary ridge on snow and boulders and entered a
deep, narrow basin. Ahead our way was blocked by a wall
of rock sweeping around from the buttress, but to the left
a snow gully led us onto the crest of the southeast ridge.
To our dismay this crest reared away in a frightening series of rock towers before it even reached the main buttress.
The buttress itself was an imposing sight—a wall, rather
than a ridge, of near vertical rock sweeping upwards for
1500 feet. In it were two cracks which we thought might be
climbed, but they failed to connect by about thirty feet of
smooth slab.

Dave and I had been the keenest advocates of this approach, but the more we saw of the buttress at this short
range the more we doubted the feasibility of ferrying supplies up it. We resolved at least to rub our noses on the
lower rocks and asked Angtemba and Siku to wait at the
foot of the ridge while we found ourselves doing moderately severe rock climbing. Dave proved a joy to climb with,
neat in movement, sure and rapid in belaying. Despite the
altitude of about 18,000 feet we were soon enjoying ourselves as we inched over one tower and then another.
Enjoying ourselves—but ruefully aware that we weren't
really doing much good. The towers were mighty severe for
a safe packing route, while the buttress continued to look
less inviting the closer we got. We had to admit it was
extremely unlikely that we could ever take loads up there.
We made a painstaking traverse on snow around another
tower and our determination wavered a little as we saw the
two that still separated us from the foot of the buttress. The
onset of a heavy snowfall at 2 P.M. clinched the matter.

The return to our starting point proved more dangerous
than the ascent. We lowered ourselves on a double rope to

avoid the traverse route, but soon an inch of new snow was hiding handholds and turning friction grips into slippery invitations to a long drop. The Sherpas were as relieved as we were when we finally got down. In drifting snow we trudged our way back to camp in gloomy silence. Neither of us liked the thought of the messy route above the lake, but the other door had slammed in our faces. Now we had no alternative.

We were tired after our first big day at altitude, and bad weather the next day gave us an excuse for a rest. Then, resigned to a siege on the face, we shifted camp up to the lake. Snow lay deeply here, but the overhang of a large boulder gave a clear corner for a fire. We rigged a tarpaulin into a cook tent, soon voted the smokiest cook tent of the trip. Water was easily obtained—a few blows of the ice ax cut through the ice to the lake underneath. Angtemba and Pembertarkay stayed in camp with us, but the others returned to the yak hut with instructions to spend the next few days relaying firewood and supplies.

In the morning the search for the route began. First problem was to find Peter's easy way—or any easy way—up to the ice field. Our problem was intensified by the heavy snow which concealed most of the shingle slopes that showed clearly in one of Peter's photographs. The ice field was a prominent feature about one third of the way up the face. Overhanging cliffs dropped away from its lower edge while above it the whole face leered, its ribbed nose dripping powder snow and its gullies forming deep-set, malevolent eyes. Dave and I differed as to the best way to reach this inhospitable spot. Dave favored an attack from across the lake. To his rock-climber's eye there was a route up the right-hand edge of the cliffs—a faint suggestion of gullies and ribs, and an angle at least a little under vertical. With the instincts of a snow-bred New Zealander I looked with more kindly eyes at the left-hand corner, hard above us. Here snow led out of sight behind a narrow rock rib; it was

my belief that this rib could be traversed and the short rock
wall dividing it from the ice field ascended. So we parted
forces and Dave and Angtemba set off early across the lake.

Pembertarkay and I were not so quick to leave. Mail was
expected up and I pursued delaying tactics which certainly
had Pembertarkay puzzled. We were actually setting off
from camp when a hail announced that my wait had not
been in vain. Torn between the urge to read the news and
the pressing need to get on with the reconnaissance, I
scrabbled through several letters, scrawled a note, and
rushed off. The other letters, still unread, were burning a
hole in my pocket, and it is a tribute to the excitement of
the day that they were unread yet when evening saw us
back in camp.

A few hundred feet above camp the snow slope was
blocked by a 20-foot rock step, breached only by two steep
ice tongues, but a few steps nicked in the left-hand tongue
took us onto a broad slope above. Progress became slow
and monotonous, but progress it was, and up a route which
would present no problems to load carriers. At length we
reached the foot of my transverse rib, but the need to
scramble onto its narrow crest was postponed by a new
possibility that had opened up before us.

Round the end of the rib tumbled a short icefall,
squeezed between containing bands of rock. If the swell of
its bulging fall could be believed, it must be coming from a
sizable stream of ice, which could only be leading down
from the ice field. Eagerly we crept up the rock at its side,
disinclined to waste time at this stage in cutting steps in the
ice. As we edged to the top of the final slab, our best hopes
were realized—before us an easy ramp of snow led up to the
lower edge of the ice field.

Breathing heavily now, we reached the ice field and sank
to rest on a convenient rock, convinced we had found
Peter's "easy scrambling" route. But it rather looked as
though Dave and Angtemba had not fared so well. Though

they had left a good hour ahead of us, they were nowhere in sight, nor could repeated yells win a response from the cliffs below. We waited half an hour, glad of the excuse, but when still they had not emerged we felt obliged to turn to the problem of where to go next.

Peter's Couloir was obvious—but equally obvious was the cone of avalanche debris which formed the apex of the ice field and which lay directly below the couloir. Since between this cone and the steep floor of the couloir there was a 40-foot pitch of loose rock—a nasty place to climb with the expectation of a new avalanche poised above—we cast our eyes elsewhere. Out to the left of the avalanche cone a narrow ramp of snow ran diagonally up as a sort of zag to the zig we had just ascended. Above there was a rock rib surprisingly free of snow. The rock was steep, but it looked firm, and with optimistic eyes we thought we could trace a traverse from the top of the rib up to the crest of the southeast ridge.

We kicked and cut our way up between two pinnacles of ice, then swung out along the ramp. We had expected to spend the entire day finding our way to the ice field, and it was an exciting bonus already to be prospecting a route beyond. Loose rock and snow made us stretch ourselves as we started up the rib, but soon we were picking our way up that true delight of a climber—rock steep enough to titillate the nerves, yet firm and easy enough to be well within the safety limit. Pembertarkay dispelled my misgivings about his climbing capabilities the instant he started up the first awkward pitch; neat and controlled, but with a volcano of suppressed energy bubbling beneath the surface, he abounded in natural ability and was clearly enjoying himself on the sun-warmed rock as much as I was. Rope length followed rope length—here a tiny overhang extending us a bit, there an amble up broad holds caressing the nerves back to calm. It seemed too good to last, and so, of course, it was. Towards one o'clock we dodged a last pitch by

traversing an easy slab, with the depths of the couloir adding spice below, and found ourselves at the end of the good
rock.

The rib continued, but here it became snow, deep loose
snow. It was broken by a series of rock bands, yellow and
unstable-looking, and joined the crest of the southeast ridge,
far above, in a final buttress of outward-sloping rock. By
now we had had more than our ration of fine weather for
the day, and the daily storm, a feature to grow increasingly
familiar, was wrapping cold tentacles around us. With so
uncertain a conclusion to our progress I was anxious to ascend at least beyond the first rock band, from where, I
hoped, I could see the whole length of Peter's Couloir and
settle finally whether a better route lay there. But we were
at 19,000 feet now, and the soft snow sucked at our boots;
moreover, Pembertarkay, for the first and only time in my
acquaintance with him, was feeling unwell. Conditions were
thus hardly ideal for determined climbing, and my two
probes at the rock band were both repulsed. With snow
swirling round us on a rising wind we had little option but
to turn our faces back towards the distant camp.

The wet snow dealt treacherously with the route below.
Weariness added its more subtle dangers, and the taste of
defeat on the rock band was sour in my mouth. But one of
the satisfactions of mountaineering is to meet and conquer
just such retreats as this. Caution concentrated on every
step, to avoid the carelessness that tiredness can bring. The
final rock of the rib faded at length into the murk behind
us, and we slouched down the ramp to the ice field.

Here we joined the footsteps of Dave and Angtemba.
While ascending the rib we had seen them appear on the
lower lip of the ice field, conjured up from nowhere in the
space between one downward glance and another. On
reaching camp we heard their story. They had fought their
way to the ice field by climbing that was as difficult as any
we later did on the mountain, up a corner of holdless rock

and rotten snow. At several points Dave had had to resort to the direct aid of pitons to get past smooth slabs. It was with relief that they saw us far above when they emerged onto the ice, for they assumed, correctly, that only by an easy route could we have raced them. Dave was full of praise for Angtemba's skill, and our liking for the Sherpas was now matched by a healthy respect for their climbing ability.

Nonetheless it was obvious that if we were to push through the route Pembertarkay and I had prospected, we would have to fix a formidable amount of rope to make it feasible for loads. Dave and I lay awake that night discussing how best to go about this task. The 500-foot rolls of manila held frightening prospects of a tangle, and cautious uncoiling would be needed to prevent a mess. There was another problem too. Looking up from camp we estimated (wrongly) that the point I had reached with Pembertarkay was halfway between the ice field and the crest of the ridge. The upper section clearly was steep and exposed, with snow I already knew to be loose. Should we proceed to fix ropes on the portion climbed, or should we first prove the whole route? Our descent in the storm had been unpleasant enough for us to feel that a roped lower section would be a real safety factor while we were tackling the upper slopes. But how wasted would be all the effort of putting the rope there if the route had to be abandoned. I went to sleep to dream uneasily of falling hundreds of feet in an endless tangle of rope.

Dave and I set off next morning carrying in turn one 500-foot coil of manila. We intended to experiment with rope fixing and also to complete the route to the ridge—so excessive was our naïve optimism. Although only 20 pounds or so, the coil served to break our rhythm as we trudged up the 1200 feet to the foot of the rib, and it became a dangerous out-pulling hump as we commenced the steep climbing. We dumped the coil 250 feet up and climbed an-

other 250 feet leading out the rope behind. We fastened the
end securely to a well-driven piton and felt a certain sense
of relief at having our escape off the mountain assured.

We continued up the enjoyable pitches of the preceding
day, this time with clouds already moving in. Our highest
point was reached in the first flurries of snow, and our hopes
of reaching the ridge that day melted dismally into the
grayness. Some careful balancing round the outside of a
snow-covered boulder avoided the rock step I had failed on,
but whether the move was really difficult or not I am at a
loss to say. Almost all the initial leads on this route seemed
very difficult at the time, but then nearly all were climbed
in bad weather and conditions. (Repeated many times later
with the fixed ropes in place, they were hard indeed to
identify as the groping pitches they had once been. Fixed
ropes can change the most formidable of routes into "an easy
day for a lady.")

Above the rock band was more soft snow. All around us
falling snow whistled past on a breath-searing wind. Feet
were cold, hands were cold and the day was already well
along. There was no argument about turning back. The
rock was already coated with snow and we rappelled the
worst pitch down to the waiting rope. Heaving the remnants
of the coil down the mountain was grand fun. One, two,
three and away it careered down the steep rock, bouncing
its diminishing bulk off projections and down gullies. We
descended hand over hand, impressed by the ease with
which a fixed rope eliminates awkward moves. Still, we
stomped back to camp feeling less than pleased with the
day's meager gains.

The next day we fared no better as far as upward progress went. With Angtemba and Pembertarkay this time we
again reached our top point to coincide with the onset of
the storm. Once again Pembertarkay and I were caught in
a difficult position. To our left was a possible route into the
gut which snaked up to the ridge crest. Above us the rib we

were on steepened into a further rock band, disappeared beyond, and then burst into view again in a final buttress that clearly offered no route. We had to get off this rib soon. From camp we had favored the lower traverse to the left, now beside us. But from here this looked so awful that I was eager despite the weather to see if there wasn't an easier way off somewhere on or above the next rock band. Dave and Angtemba were busy securing the rope on the rocks below. The two Sherpas each had carried a coil up, and the fixed line already ran right down to the ramp. Since the disappearance of the sun it had been an unpleasant task fumbling with the stiff folds of rope and hammering in cold pitons. We were equipped for much colder temperatures than these but the damp mist and wet snow made us thoroughly miserable and in a mood for going home. "I'll just have a brief look up here," I yelled and turned quickly before the others could protest.

The hoped-for traverse on the rock band came up against an awkward corner which threatened to push me off the mountain. With Pembertarkay belaying me from below, and shivering with the damp cold, I scrambled back and tried a direct route up the edge of the gully. Smooth plates of rock were coated with snow and not at all easy, but after a long hesitation over a final difficult pitch I reached the top of the band. It was small gain for my efforts. I could with difficulty peer up at a steep rib of snow—all beyond was lost in the mist—but I could decide nothing on the merits of the alternative traverses. I decided to fix a rope to this top point and banged in a piton, hitched the climbing rope around it and rappelled down to collect the end of the manila. The effort of reclimbing the rope was the final straw in an unsatisfactory day. I attached the manila and then we groped our way back to camp.

In the last two storm-racked days we had gained only about 400 feet and along a doubtful route. Dave and I, keen to prove ourselves on our first Himalayan assignment, had

had wistful dreams of pushing through a route and establishing an assault camp before any of the others joined us. The two days had dashed these dreams, and we were now glad of the knowledge that reinforcements were at hand. Mike Gill and Murray Ellis had moved up to Base Camp while we were on the mountain that day, and were to join us at Lake Camp on the morrow. We needed no discussion to declare a rest day to welcome them.

"It's time to put a camp on the ice field," was their comment when we told them of our doings. Dave and I had often discussed this move during the frustrating days just past. Dave felt it to be "unaesthetic" and verging on an admission of weakness to spatter so small a mountain with camps; while I, lazily hating the daily repetition of the climb to the ice shelf, was all for putting in as many camps as would lessen our labor. With the vote now three to one, Dave's scruples were overruled.

The following night the isolation of the ice shelf was broken by three small crouching tents. They crouched because obviously they felt that this was no place for tents to be. Concerned about avalanche danger and rockfall from the face above, we had occupied three gasping hours in digging a small platform under a slight overhang of rock. We now felt this to be a reasonably safe camp, though something about the heartiness with which we voiced this feeling might have produced suspicion in an impartial onlooker. Safe or not, the object of the camp was to get us to the ridge next day.

The vigor of the new arrivals and the beneficent effect of two easy days on Dave and me combined to create formidable determination as we set off up the fixed ropes. It was the ridge or bust! Wishing to travel light, and yet wanting to consolidate any gains we might make, we carried several hundred-foot lengths of the light nylon climbing rope—while above, at the top point, most of one of the manila coils was still unused. Reaching the foot of the last

23. Timber was carried up from the forests below for the Pangboche School. Here, barefoot Sherpa is pitsawing

24. Marking off the site

25. Grunting, groaning in a snowstorm, the expedition members raise the central ridgepole

26. A long and colorful procession awaits the head lama of Thyangboche

27. The expedition leader walks the ridge of Pangboche School, as Everest looms behind

28. In best dress and with parents to make their marks, the pupils finally enroll

29. Giant trumpets herald the opening

30. With thick rock walls and marvelous American windows, Pangboche School stands as symbol of many hopes

31. Woman on march with her child
   " 'With all respect, sahib, we know you have little to teach us in strength
and toughness. . . . But knowledge for our children—that we would like to
see!' "

32. Khumjung artist at work on vivid depiction of deity

33. Cook boy Ang Passang

34. Mingmatsering, expedition sirdar

35. Sherpa child who became Louise Hillary's favorite

36. A Sherpa ancient wearing the golden hat he treasures most highly. "Few of us had failed to learn something from the character and temperament of the men themselves, their hardiness and their cheerfulness; their vigor and loyalty; and their freedom from our civilized curse of self-pity."

step I had climbed, we were again faced with the question: when we should traverse left? From the lake all had agreed to undo the final length of rope and take the lower traverse. Once more, however, this traverse looked terrifying broadside-on—soft snow hanging by the whiskers of its crystals to the slabby rock it barely covered.

"That rope of yours looks O.K. from here," Mike suggested, and he and I went up it to try the higher traverse.

We had developed a habit of attaching ourselves to the fixed rope by a running carabiner without roping ourselves one to another. We now found the tiny platform at the top of the rope too cramped a place to rope up. So Mike pushed on round the corner. There were anxious noises as he grappled with the bank of snow above, but then he reached a rock belay and dropped me a rope.

I joined him, dragging the end of manila after me. We were none too early, for the cloud, inevitably, was closing in. But at least we had some visibility. What it revealed was not enormously encouraging. We still had before us a gully of soft snow over uncertain rock, the whole at the most unlikely angle and smelling of avalanche. But the snow seemed deep enough to form a track in, while knobbles of rock poking through at intervals promised avalanche-proof belays. With no better alternative in sight, Mike loosed a "Here goes" into the gale and set off across the gully.

It was painstaking work. The snow was of that consistency which flows round and envelops the foot, refusing to consolidate at all into some form of step. There was nothing for it but to ladle oceans of snow out of the way to form a semblance of a path, watching the while with a pessimistic eye as the dislodged snow slid down 20 or 30 feet to disappear over a sudden drop. Mike was superb—untiring with his ax, so neat in his movements that he seemed scarcely to touch the shaky track he was constructing. A rock island halfway across gave him brief respite, and he used it to gain easy height. Then it was hew and shovel for another fifteen gasping minutes until the rock at the top of the far side was gained.

Here he found a narrow wedge of rock and sat astride it to belay me up. Breathing heavily, for even with the track the snow was hard work, I passed him the end of the manila and edged round underneath his rock. This had already, he mournfully informed me, changed from wedge to razor edge, and was causing pain to a fundamental part of his anatomy. "Don't let me hurry you," he said, "but it's down to the bone already." I was too tired to spare more than a sympathetic grunt.

Beyond was a gully depressingly like the one we had just crossed. I waded out into it, flailing anxiously with my ax and expecting every second that I and the snow would slide away over its abrupt lip. My frantic flounderings brought me through to the underlying rock and twice I was able to drive in pitons for running belays—and as quieters for raw nerves. I felt as if I were on an impossibly steep sand dune in moving, thigh-deep sand. After a very long time I gained the far side and tied thankfully onto a boulder.

We were now poised beside and just above the nasty part of the gully which led to the crest of the ridge. The near vertical wall of the gully gave little chance of descending directly into it, so Mike cut up the dividing rib, on firm snow at last, until he reached the rock wall in which it culminated. The traverse on this wall was tricky with crampons on; but it was a pleasure to be on rock again, and it brought us into the kindlier upper portion of the gully.

Dave and Murray meanwhile had had the thankless task of adjusting and finally securing the assorted lengths of rope with which Mike and I were festooning the mountain. We had long since used up the manila and started on the climbing ropes, and one of our concerns was whether we would reach the ridge or run out of rope first. We continued up through the clinging snow of the upper gully, paying out our diminishing ball like parsimonious old ladies knitting for the local church bazaar. Our arrival at the ridge, the culmination of days of hard and dangerous effort, was in many ways an anticlimax. Visibility was nil, hands and feet were cruel lumps of cold, and our last rope—the one Mike and I had been using as a climbing rope—failed by about five feet to make the grade. Still, we were there!

Murray and Dave joined us. Stamping our feet and blinking our eyes, we tried by will power to wrench a cleft in the drifting curtain of snow. Though well above the buttress that Dave and I had dallied with seemingly so long ago, we had a shrewd notion we still had at least two steep sections of ridge between us and the plateau. But their nature we had to guess, for a messy crest of rock and snow disappearing into the mist was all we could see.

Nonetheless the track below gave satisfaction. The route so far was a spectacular one for load carrying—steep rock followed by exposed snow traverses. And yet the fixed ropes made it safe and reasonable, as we found to our delight when we were able to whisk down to Camp I in an hour. There had been some heartburn in the camp over these fixed ropes, particularly on the part of Dave and Tom. The specialized rock-climbing of the States has given rise to tight rules about what's done or not done, and trussing your mountain up like a hog-tied steer is evidently on the latter list. But as Murray, Mike and I imagined moving loads breathlessly up this rock and incohesive snow, and contemplated the deathtrap into which an innocent storm could turn this face, our milder New Zealand consciences had little trouble in condoning the practice.

Back at camp Angtemba and Pembertarkay had reproachful news for us. They had been peacefully inside their tent when a rock the size of a human head rudely joined them. Reflecting philosophically that this was no more than one could expect with clumsy sahibs above, they had already repaired the tent damage, and were themselves unhurt, bar shaken nerves. But Camp I's security rating had dropped several points so far as they were concerned.

We were full of plans that night, for we really believed we had the back of the task broken. Whatever the ridge might throw at us could hardly be worse than what we had waded through that day; and nothing remained but the establishment of a camp on the plateau, and then the final assault. The question mark, we thought, was provided more by those below than by the difficulties above. Should we suggest that the four of us present push on with the assault, or should we in decency call the others up for their turn at the high end of the fun? Pondering this question, little knowing how useless the events of next morning would make the mental effort involved, we fell into the refreshing sleep that is the lot of those who consider they have behind them a day's hard work well done.

"* * * * *." The voice heatedly competing with the static was undoubtedly Ed's, but the content of his speech was not easy to hear. Crouched round the radio in Mike's and Murray's tent, breakfast over and boots ready to go and investigate the ridge, we looked at each other for inspiration. The motive for our next move is still in dispute, but I stoutly maintain that Mike and I, at least, honestly believed Ed to have said something about continuing the assault. Doubtless Freud has words to explain this belief, but there it was. So Mike, grabbing the speaker, uttered his famous lines: "Understand you to say go ahead with assault. Please confirm."

No static in the world could hide Ed's answer—indeed it may well have bypassed the radio altogether and boomed in from Pangboche on natural resonance alone. "Negative! *negative*. Message is return to Pangboche today."

A terse silence reverberated over the air as we digested this news and found it unwholesome. Someone finally had the foolhardiness to admit that the message had been received, but lengthy minutes passed before we made any move.

Prevented by the bad circuit from sharing with us the reasons for his sudden withdrawal command, Ed was the object of a certain amount of unjust comment as we prepared to descend. In an excess of frustrated energy we enlarged the platform by two hours' digging before repitching one tent and storing all the gear in it. Then a three-hour romp landed us in the midst of the school-building activity at Pangboche.

It needed only the news of the troubled doings there, which had precipitated our descent, to make us feel pretty foolish about our indignation. But the saga of Pangboche School is not our concern here. Suffice it to say that not only was there urgent need for all hands to complete the school, but also the weather was so foul during the whole week or so we were down that we were lucky to be off the mountain. Only by racing across to the vantage point of the school site before breakfast could we manage to see the mountain and examine our next problems through the glasses; for the rest of the day, though Everest and Ama Dablam and Kangtega often smiled in the sun until midmorning, Taweche glowered sullenly behind its swirling cloud.

Nor was it any better the day we set off towards the mountain again. Ed was with us and we were eager to show him the route; but glimpses through rare breaks in the cloud were all we were allowed, and the slender lines of the fixed ropes were difficult to distinguish.

At the yak pasture, officially still the Base Camp, Phudorje and Siku were in residence guarding the equipment. Dark doings had been reported from this camp during the week we were down below—Taweche and his friend the yeti (Abominable Snowman) had frequently growled and groaned at the terrified Sherpas in the night, and once the spirit of the god had even chased them fleeing across the black hillside, as torn trousers and tattered down jackets testified. For these and other more mundane reasons we decided to transfer everything to the lake camp. Ed was along to help with the shift as a break from organizing the schools. Loads were hoisted onto willing shoulders—the Sherpas', not ours—and in the inevitable snowfall we panted up to the lake and dug in the camp.

With one of the big tents, a remodeled cook tent, and plenty of firewood this camp was now to become quite a comfortable base from which the Sherpas would operate. Camp I, on the ice shelf, was not favorably regarded by many after the rock incident, and was to be occupied only by climbing parties working on the route. Tom Frost was now sufficiently recovered from a bad dose of glandular fever to make it up to the lake, and we could call down from Camp I by radio whenever supplies or load carriers were needed.

Mike, Dave, Angtemba, and I moved up next day to dig out Camp I. If we needed proof of the bad weather of the past week it was amply provided by the sight of the tent, collapsed and torn under the mass of new snow. We thought ruefully of our route above, doubtless also heavily buried.

The task of clearing the route fell to Dave and Mike. Next morning they rapidly scaled the ropes to the ridge crest, which they reached by noon. Gray skies for once lay haughtily above, not around, the mountain, and for the first day on record no snow fell. Fastening more rope as they went, they kicked and shuffled their way up the loose ridge till they came up against the first of the two rock steps we had seen from Pangboche. It was an unkind slab, smooth and steep, with a dusting of snow to make pressure holds useless. Belayed by Mike, Dave edged round to the left, finding himself balancing on the side of the ridge with a yawning space beneath his feet. His nerves straining to detect the first moment of a snowslide, he crept cautiously on until he reached a stance below a rock gully which offered a chance of topping the slab.

Mike passed him and tackled this gully. A vertical start swelled into a small but decided overhang before receding into a sloping groove. Loose rock added danger. A pleasant problem at sea level on a sunny afternoon, but anguished effort on a gray day at 20,000 feet. Mike hammered two pitons home and swung himself up on them, up and out and over the overhang, to reach the groove beyond. The powder snow made this wildly slippery, but ten feet of delicate balance and he was at the top of the slab.

Dave grunted up, and was given the freedom of the mountain by Mike's wave at the next section of the ridge. Never a waster of words, Dave transferred the fixed rope from his waist to a stout piton before replying. The downward-sweeping comment of his hand met with Mike's complete approval, for it was already 4 P.M. They made haste to descend, comforted by the foolish hope that Angtemba and I would have the meal waiting for them.

Mike and I reached the first rock step next day and I had difficulty with Mike's pitch even with the aid of the rope. By 1 P.M. we were at the second step and found it no less severe and about three times as high as the first. A 100-foot slab, its small holds and sheer angle again made direct assault inadvisable. Mike tied himself firmly to a rock and announced with equal firmness that the honor was mine. So I began a cautious flanking movement over the exposed face on the left. Soft snow over slabs and ribs forced me round under an uncompromising right-angled overhang. The mountain's obvious intent was to rid itself of this insolent trespasser; but with pitons to help I crept over a flaw in the overhang and into an easier, snow-filled gully. Thence —slowly, for I was increasingly weary—to the top of the slab. A frozen Mike informed me that the lead had taken one and a half hours.

Snow was falling again as I hauled up and fastened a

wire ladder to make a route up the slab. Mike did the nearest thing possible at that altitude to shinnying up the ladder, and arrived panting beside me. Unbelievably, we were still not at the plateau, but instead were clinging to the foot of a steep snow slope which rose some 150 feet to a sharp peaklet. A corniced 20 feet of translucent snow ridge then wavered left to connect, not even then with the plateau proper, but with at least a possible campsite on a small lip below the plateau. Varying ice and soft snow wrung grunts of frustration from Mike as he alternatively cut and plowed a tired trail up the slope. From a ledge just short of the crest we could assure ourselves about the campsite, and, as the 20 feet of cornice threatened to benight us, we turned down again with the plateau still untrodden. Our cold fingers irritatingly fumbled rope and wire. We fixed the lower step with a ladder, and then gravity dragged us down the rope and deposited us in a heap at Camp I.

Storm without, discussion within, raged next day, the one confining us to the tents and giving ample time for the other. The point at issue was whether to take advantage of the next fine day to complete the route and establish an assault camp in one move—Dave's and my view—or whether to spend it completing and consolidating the route only, which Mike held to be the sensible course. Eventually numerical democracy triumphed, and we spent some miserable hours outside in a final check of assault-camp loads, snow drifting into kitbags and down necks. A radio call to Tom arranged for four Sherpas to be with us early to carry the loads.

That the next morning was nondescript is the kindest thing one could say of it. But we had breakfast in case the weather improved, and by the time the Sherpas turned up there were enough good signs to entice us away. There followed a totally exhausting day. The Sherpas went up the steep slopes magnificently, but with their 40-pound loads had to be helped on some pitches, a tiring performance when straining to ascend oneself. The wire ladders were too difficult for backpacking loads, though the Sherpas would willingly have tried, and we decided to send the men back from below them—all except Angtemba, who was the fourth for the assault party. From there on, we started to haul and carry the loads ourselves. Forty-pound loads increase alarmingly in size as they are transferred from Sherpa backs to the end of a rope dragged up steep rock, and even the first-step haul finished me. Dave's annoyance was justified, therefore, when Mike and I, on the flimsy excuse of having had a lot of ice experience in New Zealand, shamefully left him and Angtemba to pull the second step alone while we went on to finish the last section of the route. Poor Dave, with his quiet ways, suffered more than once on this expedition from our brash assertiveness, but bore up commendably under the strain.

The corniced ridge was no joke: unstable bulges of ice, with the drop on both sides hardly bearing contemplation. Mike edged unhappily out onto it. Laying about him with his ax in a last spasm of tired energy, he cut and kicked six to eight feet off the top to form a 12-inch track, albeit a somewhat bumpy one. A rope gave it an illusion of security. Near the end of our tether now, we relayed the loads up from the rock step, and stomped out a platform to take the two small red tents.

The tortuous route up had gained us a spectacular campsite. A narrow ledge of semihorizontal snow squatted beneath the plateau lip, and ended 10 feet beyond the tents in an ice cliff brooding over a 3000-foot face. The mist cleared, revealing the peaks nearby—Everest (climbed by the American party a few days before), Lhotse, Nuptse, Ama Dablam, Kangtega—and leaving us with an awed sense of height and loneliness. Slowly the sun dipped into a red bath of cloud, as indifferent to our wonder as to our weariness. The stark world of black and white leaped into brilliant color, only to die away into the cruel monotone of a Himalayan night. Human dots in immensity of blackness, we turned uneasily away, and between the confining walls of the tents acted out once again man's great self-deception—the creation of a world small enough for him to comprehend.

With every fiber strained to the task of setting up this assault camp, we had devoted little thought to the problems we might meet on the slopes above. To be honest, we still were thinking that once the plateau was reached the peak was as good as ours. Not even our weariness that night could completely bury a fierce confidence. "We've been battering away for weeks to construct that damn route," ran our thoughts, "and now only straight climbing remains." Alas for our folly—we should have known by then that Taweche was not one to relent even at this late stage.

With an exhausting day just over, we planned a reconnaissance first, with an assault the following day. Mike and Dave moved off about 7:30 A.M., while I groveled with altitude sickness. They hit the first trouble right away—powder snow over ice. Surmounting it with ill-humored effort, they moved out across the long-dreamed-of plateau, which is quite a sizable glacier shelf draining the south face of the summit cone. As for this face, now in full view, there seemed little doubt that the right-hand corner was the best proposition. But even this favored corner was extremely steep and ended in a huge ice bulge. The gentle rise across the plateau was heavy with powder snow, and they knew that a similar depth on the face would mean defeat, for the danger of avalanche would be enormous. Gone was the exultation of the previous night; it had to be replaced with a grim determination to test that snow and to cut steps as high as possible on the mountain to speed the climb next day. The bergschrund splitting the plateau from the slopes above was crossed quite easily over a bridge of deep snow. Their tentative probe up the face forced them to scrape off a thick layer of powder snow before they could get through to a more stable surface underneath and cut steps in snow that was sometimes firm and sometimes soft. As the slopes steepened to the average angle of the face, however, the depth of powder snow decreased. For the first time that day a glimmer of confidence returned. They even considered the possibility of attempting the summit there and then, but regretfully turned down the idea in deference to the absence of Angtemba and myself. By the time they retraced their steps to camp there was a line of steps slanting some 200 feet up the face to show for their efforts.

Meanwhile I had not been allowed to suffer in peace. Murray and Phil were at Base Camp, and, as planned, were that day bringing up more supplies for Camp II. Moving with the same free speed that had the previous day carried them from Khumjung to the lake in one day, they were hailing me from the wire ladders at the early hour of 9 A.M. Right in behind them, oblivious of the forty pounds or more on his back, was the brown grin of Phudorje. Pangboche Tenzing, Karmatila and Hakpanurbu soon arrived. The painful task of hauling and relaying the loads was completed at last. Murray still had not had enough, and went up onto the plateau to see where the others were, while Phil and I produced a meal of sorts. When Dave and Mike returned, Phil and Murray descended, much impressed by the lonely splendor of the assault camp.

That night only Angtemba remained disinterested as we cautiously jockeyed for positions on the leading rope for the assault. The problem was that on that steep face there would be no chance to change the order of the ropes, and the one who led off would remain in the lead till the summit ridge was reached. Following up in prepared steps has not the same appeal as the virgin thrill of cutting the steps, and none of us was eager to make up the second rope with Angtemba. Democracy being powerless in so even a division, we resorted to the ancient principle of lots. The toss of the coin decreed that Dave and Mike would depart first, with Angtemba and me to follow. We were to give the first pair plenty of head start and catch up with them near the top of the face, the alternative being long hours of waiting and deluges of ice and snow as the staircase was fashioned.

Dave and Mike were away by about 6 A.M. The altitude still hung heavily at the pit of my stomach as Angtemba and I followed about 7:30, and the plateau was a weary slog. Ahead we could see the others striking up beyond their prepared steps. The slope had deteriorated again, and with enormous labor they were shoveling off up to a foot of unstable snow before chipping steps in the varying surface below. Shaft firmly embedded, one would belay while the other swept and cut a rope length up, often taking over half an hour, so tiring was the work. Then he would sink his shaft—our one blessing was that good shaft belays were lacking only once—and the first would move up to him, then on past for a further rope length. The exposure increased as they inched up the face, and the angle was so sharp that their noses all but rubbed in the snow.

The Summit

It took from 7 A.M. to 1 P.M. to defeat those 800 feet, but at length we were all crouched together on a tiny platform of ice below the bulge. Ice pitons were Mike's belay as Dave crept round a corner into a slight gully which breached the overhang of the bulge. He was beyond the "safety net" of the plateau now, and swayed on tiny nicks above a dizzy 4000-foot plunge of snow. The gully ended in a vertical cornice, but some delicate balancing, a final groaning heave, and Dave at length pulled himself through onto the summit ridge of Taweche. We hastened to join him—then stood appalled.

Taweche had played her cards well. No one could accuse

her of trying to deceive us with gentle lower slopes, but we had imagined her strongest trumps had been played when she threw at us first the face, then the rock steps, then the ultimate slopes we had just ascended.

We were standing on the broad, almost flat top of the ice bulge. Its gentle snow continued for perhaps 20 yards more. But beyond that all hell had been let loose. A tenuous ridge twined up for 200 feet to the summit ice bulge—rearing soft-snow cornices which, so far as we could tell, were undercut on both sides. I think there was little doubt in anyone's mind after the first glance, but we had to make a gesture if but for form. Fearfully we crept a few yards out along the ridge. On the one side the snarling cornices overhung the plateau; on the other, steep soft snow itching to avalanche; then nothing but remote yak pastures 6000 feet below. Mike and I were more than willing to raise our hats to our adversary for a neat stymie. We were quite sure there were only one-way tickets available for that stretch of ridge, for the hanging snow on the right made impossible the low traverse necessary to keep below the cornices. Dave alone seemed keen to prod a last defiant ax at the mountain. Whether he really thought we could inch along the top of the cornices will never be known, for Mike and I, able to offer only a farcical token of a belay from our knee-deep stance in steep snow, rather shortly declined to remain attached to the rope if he went farther.

Cautiously placing at our highest spot—an estimated three to four rope lengths and some 150 to 200 vertical feet from the top—the prayer flags entrusted to us by the head lama of Thyangboche Monastery, we slouched back to the comparative safety of the ice bulge. Moodily chomping a bite of food, we sought in silence, each in his own way, to reconcile ourselves to the defeat. To pretend we were not disappointed would be idle, but Mike hit an answering chord when eventually he quietly said, "You know, I think in some ways it's better not to have violated so beautiful a summit." And indeed, even in the moment of our defeat it was difficult to begrudge the mountain its victory. We had been narrowly beaten in a hard clean fight, and the overworked cliché about the relative importance of playing well and winning for once seemed to have some meaning.

This did not quite complete our struggles with Taweche. Leading up from the left-hand side of the plateau was an appallingly steep ridge which we thought might be worth investigating. After a period of very confusing activity Murray Ellis, Tom Frost, Pembertarkay and I re-established Camp II. It took but a few hours the next day to finish the story. Struggling up to the plateau in new knee-deep snow, we gained a spot with an unimpeded view of the face and the left-hand ridge of the summit cone. It was horrifyingly difficult. Steeper and half as long again as the face we had ascended previously, it was fluted with knobbly festoons of ice and overhung by the same cornices we had declined to dally with before. As fresh mist and snow swept in on a stinging wind, we turned and crept back to camp.

To Tom, Pembertarkay and me fell the dismal task of reducing the camp to orderly loads and removing the long fixed ropes. The Sherpas, summoned by radio, were waiting below the bottom ladder long before we had dragged and lowered the loads to them. Tom and I gathered ourselves for one last effort. We were unwilling to leave Taweche cluttered with pitons and odd bits of rope, so for hours we wrestled with wire ladders, battled with python-like coils of manila and beat peevishly at stubborn pitons. Many long hours elapsed before the final rope was dropped onto the snow ramp and the last pitons removed. An hour later we were all safely off the mountain.

It had been a long battle. Over a month had elapsed since Dave and I had first set foot on Taweche—a month of continuous bad weather, unrelenting mountain, and ultimate defeat. Of pleasure, in the weak meaning of the word, there had been practically none; of pain, cold, weariness and nausea, more than ample share. Yet not one of us would have missed a moment of our experience and Taweche will remain one of our vivid memories when lesser and easier mountains have long been forgotten.

—*Jim Wilson*

Chapter 6

MEDICAL CLINIC

IT IS commonly accepted that the isolated mountain valleys of the Himalayas are Shangri-Las where there is no
sickness and people live on forever. Such, alas, is not the
case—or certainly not in the various Himalayan regions I
have visited. Ill health and disease are just as common as
in civilization, but there are no medical aids or drugs to
combat them and people recover through their own natural
resistance or they die. A high percentage of children never
reach maturity. Most of the Sherpa mothers with two or
three children have actually borne four, five or six. And the
number of young mothers who don't survive childbirth is
appallingly high. During the course of one of my expeditions two of my ten best Sherpas had their wives die in
childbirth.

Much of this is due to dirty conditions and is aggravated
by a complete lack of any sort of medical knowledge. But
the rigors of the woman's life in this society must also play
an important part. There's no time to rest and recuperate.
Work must go on: there is food to be prepared, fields to be
tilled, firewood collected and huge loads carried. A good
example of this is the case of Mrs. Khunjo Chumbi, wife of
one of the Khumjung headmen. Three years ago when
Queen Elizabeth came on a state visit to Nepal, Mrs.
Chumbi was determined to go to Katmandu despite the fact
that her sixth baby was due at any moment. With a 180-
mile walk in front of her she made only one concession to
her condition—she reduced the work load she was carrying

to a modest 30 pounds. Four days' march and sixty miles from her destination Mrs. Chumbi was forced to take shelter in a tiny tumbledown wayside cottage. She emerged an hour later holding her new son, then continued the march towards Katmandu. The journey was completed without further delay and the baby was well nourished even though his mother had been walking fourteen or fifteen miles a day.

After one night in the city it became apparent that all was not well with Mrs. Chumbi. She was having severe afterbirth pains, so we rushed her to the local mission hospital. Here an examination showed that she was still carrying the placenta. Doctors quickly acted to rectify this problem. Within twenty-four hours Mrs. Chumbi appeared smiling and happy, dressed in her best clothes, at the British Embassy garden party and achieved her desire, to meet Queen Elizabeth, "the headman of many villages."

Mrs. Chumbi's experience ended quite happily, thanks to prompt medical treatment (and her own remarkable toughness), but in most cases there would have been only one result—the mother's death. In Sherpaland the "weaklings" die quickly; only the tough and hardy can hope to survive.

Himalayan expeditions have built up a tradition of giving medical attention to all who come asking for it. We went even farther than this. With two doctors and a large supply of drugs we established a medical clinic in Khumjung for a six-month period. Our aim was not only to give immediate medical treatment to the Sherpas, but also to carry out a wider investigation with a view to establishing more long-range medical aid in the future.

From the time the walk in started our two doctors were kept busy. I remember particularly the evening we spent in Junbesi. One of our young Sherpas, a delightful boy, had a badly swollen leg and was in considerable pain. Phil Houghton decided he must operate. We laid the boy on a tarpaulin spread on the ground. All our porters and the

entire population of the village clustered around as Phil cut
the leg open and removed large quantities of fluid and
blood. The poor lad was absolutely terrified and convinced
he was about to die. Desmond held his hand and kept up a
continual stream of encouraging comments, but we were
all mighty glad when the job was finished. As the boy was
showing all the signs of shock—less from the operation than
from the outspoken predictions of disaster by the Junbesi
villagers—I put up an extra tent, and the pale and shaking
lad was slipped into a sleeping bag. Well sedated, he was
left to sleep peacefully away from prying eyes. By morning
he was already on the road to recovery.

Meanwhile the doctors were carrying on with a variety
of patients: a boy bitten by a dog; various old ladies with
pains in their tummies and chests; a singularly robust woman
who said she hadn't slept for twenty-four days; and, perhaps
saddest of all, a young couple with an eighteen-month-old
child suffering from TB of the spine. I can still see the
father's large, sad eyes filling with hopelessness as he was
told that the only chance was a hospital—how could he
spare the time and money for this? Being a doctor in such
an area must, despite many frustrations, be a rewarding
occupation. Certainly no one can bring more immediate
blessing or see more spectacular results for his efforts. These
people have built up no resistance to antibiotics even in
their simpler forms, and the cures that can be effected at
times verge on the miraculous.

Problems which are no longer expected in Western society
are frequently met. In the village of Jiri there is a small but
efficient Swiss hospital where I remember seeing a man
being treated for severe lacerations. His left arm and shoulder had been badly mauled, but despite this he had walked
several days from his village to get treatment. I was particularly impressed with his cheerful, smiling face and his will-
ingness to bandy jokes about the injuries, which I discovered had been inflicted by a leopard. The man had been

grazing his animals on a hilly pasture when he noticed the animal crouching to leap on a straying calf. Without thought to the consequences he had snatched out his fearsome knife, the kukri, and, shouting loudly to attract its attention, headed at a rush towards the leopard. The animal was angry at being diverted from its meal and made a tremendous spring to meet the man halfway. As the leopard's wide-open jaws approached him, the farmer quickly thrust his left hand down its throat and submitted to having his arm and side scratched to ribbons while he methodically hacked the leopard's head off with his kukri. The leopard fell dead, and the man collected his cows and drove them back to safety before worrying about any treatment for his wounds. A mixture of ashes and dung plastered on had stopped the bleeding, and he had walked for two days to get to the hospital. The thing that impressed me most was that he didn't really think he'd done anything remarkable. "What else could I have done, sahib?" Obviously the thought of just running off and leaving the calf to its fate hadn't entered his mind. It was good to know that such a brave and resourceful man was getting adequate treatment.

Hospital in a Gompa

The clinic at Khumjung started in a 10×10-foot tent. The pressure was on immediately with our major involvement in the smallpox epidemic. It soon became apparent that we needed more room for the surgical jobs and more shelves for the multitude of pills, drugs, and bandages. Mingmatsering suggested we take over one of the guest rooms in the Khumjung Gompa. The room was dusty and dirty, with old mud-plastered walls and an uneven floor. But it seemed essentially sound in structure, and the glassless window framed a tremendous view of Tamserku, with its saw-toothed ice ridges sharp against the eastern sky.

After consultation with the village headmen we agreed to share the costs of renovation. The village put in a solid wooden floor and a raised sleeping bench. Then they plastered the walls with fresh clay and repaired the wood-shake roof.

We, in our turn, lined the walls with bamboo matting and built a series of long shelves for the drugs and a couple of solid tables for operating purposes. We screened the sleeping bench off from the main room so the doctors could have some privacy. A wood-burning stove was installed for comfort. We enlarged the window considerably to take full advantage of the view. As we found the repaired roof still inadequate, we laid first bamboo matting over the rafters, then plastic sheeting, with wood shakes and finally heavy rocks to hold it all down. With the walls hung with Tibetan relics, a pressure lamp flooding the room with light, and the stove glowing cherry red in the corner, the two doctors relaxed in their comfortable chairs and looked at peace with the world.

One of our first patients was a strapping young Tibetan refugee. I had first noticed him at Thami, limping around most painfully, and had inquired about his disability. He was suffering from frostbite, we were told. Some months before, he had escaped to Thami with his ancient mother and his sister, a nun. After a short stay in Thami the sister had felt a deep urge to return to her nunnery, as she had heard that it was so poor, the Chinese had left it untouched. Undeterred by the winter snows on the 19,000-foot Nangpa La Pass and the possible consequences to him if he were caught, our Tibetan had left his mother in Thami and taken his sister back to her home, traveling mostly at night. On his way back over the Nangpa La he struck a bitter storm. He knew that if he stopped he would be lost. For two days he plunged on through the winter snows without rest or food until he dropped down off the glacier and struggled wearily downvalley to Thami. He staggered into the miserable tent containing his old mother and collapsed from exhaustion. He was back alive but his feet had been frostbitten in the storm.

We told the man that he must come to Khumjung for treatment, as it would be a long and tedious process if we were to save his feet. What to do with his mother was the question which worried him most. We agreed that he would come to Khumjung when he had solved this problem.

Three days later he limped into Khumjung on bloodstained feet, having done the three-hour trip in two days. He had a Tibetan boy to support him, and another refugee family was looking after his mother. For an hour Phil cleaned his blackened feet and snipped away dead and battered skin. The result was quite encouraging. The flesh underneath seemed red and healthy and if further infection could be prevented, the man might lose only a couple of toes. But it was going to take time—a lot of time.

"Can you afford accommodation in the village?" we asked.

"I have no money."

"Can you stay with friends?"

"I am a refugee. I have no friends here. I have a little food and other Tibetans will probably give me a little more."

We decided to make a home for him. Our Sherpas hacked some long poles out of the bush and I produced one of our precious tarpaulins. In the shelter of a large rock we erected a ridgepole tent and moved him into it. With his companion to collect firewood and cook his food, he could live here in reasonable comfort. We gave him some food and Tibetans in the village gave him some more. He quickly became quite a local personality and there was usually a group of friends sitting cross-legged around his fire, talking and laughing in deep, chesty tones.

After a month in Khumjung the man was making very satisfactory progress. Then one day we returned to the village and found him missing from his tent. "Where has he gone?" we asked. "A messenger came from Thami to say his old mother is dying and wants her son beside her. We told him he was a fool to walk on his injured feet but nothing would stop him. He left two hours ago, supported by his friend."

After working on these feet for a month, Phil had no intention of seeing all his work destroyed in a day. "We must have a horse for him," he said. "Couldn't we hire the headman's old nag?" After brief negotiations the horse duly turned up and was sent off after the Tibetan with strict instructions that he must ride at all times and use his feet only when absolutely necessary. Early next morning the horse arrived back in Khumjung, but no Tibetan. He sent a message: "My mother died before I could reach Thami. I am staying here for a few days to take care of her funeral. It is my duty that her pathway to the gods be made as easy as possible."

Several days later Desmond passed through Thami. He found the Tibetans' camp in mourning and our patient greatly distressed because he didn't have enough money to buy firewood to give his mother a worthy cremation. Touched by the Tibetan's very real distress, Desmond gave him twenty rupees and wished him well.

Five days later our patient arrived back in Khumjung, having walked all the way.

"Were the funeral celebrations successful?" we asked.

"Yes, sahib! The lamas came down from the Thami Gompa and told us that the money would be better spent on pujas in the monastery for the soul of my mother. For two days the lamas prayed and then we threw my mother into the Bhote River. She will be very happy at what I have done for her. Although I am sad I am well content!"

Phil examined the man's feet with some concern. They were pink and healthy and seemed unaffected by his ten-mile walk.

Although much of the medical work was the sort of thing not commonly seen in our own more hygienic society, notably diarrhea caused by most of the parasites and bacteria known to medical science—nevertheless we were surprised to find here many of the diseases that we commonly encounter in civilization. On our clinic list were patients with heart failure, many with pneumonia (we saved at least three lives with antibiotics), chronic lung disease, venereal disease, a solitary case of gallstones, and cancer. One of Phil's most regular patients was a woman of fifty-five with cancer of the breast, an ugly wound that had already spread to the glands under the arm. All we could do for her was clean and dress the sore and helplessly watch her grow thinner day by day. We couldn't even do much to ease her pain, as this would seriously have depleted our supply of drugs. Instead she had to carry on as her people had carried on for generations, suffering but not complaining.

A Land without Convalescents

Another case was nearer home. My old friend Khunjo Chumbi came to us frequently, complaining of pain in his stomach. The doctors at first thought this was a simple peptic ulcer but despite excellent medical attention at the Shanta Bawan Hospital in Katmandu, he returned to Khumjung with his pain unrelieved. Although he seemed as active as ever, yet he had begun to look ominously gaunt and we left Khumjung with the uneasy suspicion that he might well have a stomach cancer—and might not be there to greet us when we returned on our next expedition.

The most important of the killing diseases was TB; we saw it affecting lungs, joints, spines, eyes, and skin in all its many and bizarre forms. There was a lama at Thyangboche coughing up blood almost continuously; three young children in Namche had collapsed spines; a husky young Tibetan refugee and his young sister died in less than two months from the time they began to feel unwell. With a hospital and intensive treatment these lives could have been saved had the disease been caught in the early stages— but by the time they reluctantly called on us for help the sufferers were already dying.

The most impressive operation I saw Phil Houghton carry out was to sew up a damaged eyelid. The man arrived up from Namche Bazar in great distress. His eye was a gory mess. He'd been chopping firewood and a splinter had shot up and hit him in the face. With the gentle tenderness of a woman Phil carefully wiped away the blood and revealed the wound. What a sight it was—the eyelid was almost completely severed and hung by a thin bridge of skin and flesh. The eye itself was bruised and scratched but not perhaps beyond recall. With thread and needle Phil sewed the eyelid back into place, a long and difficult task. The man shook and quivered under the pain and shock, but never uttered a word. For two hours the operation went on, and by the end of it all of us watching were as tired and strained as Phil himself. "It is most important," he said, "that the eye doesn't get infected, as then I might have to remove it to prevent the other eye from being blinded as well. The thought of removing an eye under these conditions fills me with horror."

For a week or more the man came up from Namche each day for bandaging and treatment and the eye remained clean and healthy. And then we saw no more of him.

"What happened to the man with the eye?" we inquired. "He must have more treatment and drugs."

"He is much improved," we were told, "and no longer suffers any discomfort. He could delay no longer a trading trip downvalley and has departed with his family."

And that's the last we saw of him. He may have recovered or be permanently blinded, but life here is tough and the word "convalescent" is practically unknown.

As the expedition was carrying on a number of projects as well as mountaineering, there wasn't always a doctor at

37. Filling the horizon is the massive, uncompromising south face of Taweche

38. Everest sunset seen from the desolate site of our Base Camp

39. Fixed ropes leading from "Peter's Couloir" onto the northeast face of Taweche

40. Rib of soft, foot-enveloping snow below Camp II

41. Steep going up shaky track allowed no change of position

42. Pembertarkay above Camp II

43. In lonely splendor the assault camp at 20,000 feet faces Everest

44. The last 200 feet. Prayer flags are to the right

Khumjung, so medical duties had to be delegated to other expedition members. Most of the routine tasks like bandaging could be handled effectively by one of our Sherpas, Khuncha, who had shown considerable aptitude as a medical assistant. On one occasion a man recovering from pneumonia had to receive daily injections of penicillin and Bhanu Bannerjee volunteered to carry out this task. It wasn't until Bhanu was about to leave camp, equipped with hypodermic syringe and drug, that I discovered that he had never given an injection before although, as he said, "I've seen hundreds of them given—on me, when I was in hospital with frostbite!" I decided to go along for moral support—both for Bhanu and the patient.

We entered one of the larger houses in the village and found the owner huddled miserably in his blankets, obviously still far from well. At our request he sat up and bared an arm as thin as a peastick. Bhanu was somewhat taken aback. His experience was based on his own well-fleshed limbs and there seemed no scope here for the needle without scraping the bone. Undaunted, he tackled the job with determination but slowly, very slowly. Not for him the sharp, professional prod—instead the point was placed on the skin and then gently, very gently depressed. It seemed ten minutes both to the patient and to me before the needle had reached the required depth. And now, reversing the customary practice which recommends a slow ejection of the fluid into the tissues, Bhanu acted with great dispatch. He pressed the plunger most firmly and it was with difficulty the patient restrained his scream of pain. He fell back with beads of sweat on his brow and asked in broken tones, "When is the Doctor Sahib returning?" A desperate look came into his eyes when we mentioned three days' time. The man's recovery was phenomenal. We arrived next day to find him working around the house and protesting that he was now well—but nothing could stop Bhanu's newfound medical enthusiasm and once again the ritual was carried to its agonizing conclusion. The third day Bhanu arrived to find the house empty of its owner.

"My husband told me to say he has gone to see his yaks," the wife said, "and that they are far away, very far away!"

Hazards of the Mountains

The Sherpas live in such steep, rough country that inevitably our doctors had to deal with fractures resulting from slips or falls. Under normal conditions when there is no medical care a compound fracture can easily result in infection and death. The Sherpas appear to have no skill at setting fractures, and distorted limbs are the usual result. There is also danger to be experienced from creatures such as the Himalayan bear. I have seen a number of men deformed and scarred after an encounter with a bear, although of course they were lucky to survive at all. It has been a custom in the past for the Sherpas to blame unexplained deaths by assault on the Abominable Snowman, but with the new generation this habit appears to be disappearing. Snakes, too, can be encountered in the lower valleys. We came upon a young boy with a swollen arm and puncture marks. He had been cutting grass and a snake had bitten him. We had no antivenin and as the boy had already survived for two and one half hours and was capable of walking around unaided, we guessed that the snake couldn't have been a particularly poisonous one. We gave him some aspirins and sent him off to bed—then gave his parents a severe lecture about not repeating again and again "My son is dying! My son is dying!" as the boy was already completely terrified. In the twelve years I have been visiting the Himalayas I have seen perhaps a dozen snakes and killed two of them, one with an umbrella and one with a large rock. The Sherpas are terrified of all snakes and it is doubtful whether they are able to distinguish the really venomous from the harmless varieties.

My sirdar, Mingmatsering is as solid and sensible a man as you would find anywhere. For some days he hadn't been looking well and was far from his normal dynamic self. We suggested he see our doctors and get some treatment. He agreed to do this but shook his head in doubt all the same. "I am being poisoned by witchcraft, sahib! In making arrangements for the schools in the villages I must unwittingly have offended someone and he is getting his revenge." Our drugs had some effect but even by the end of the expedition Mingma hadn't completely recovered.

When we arrived back in Katmandu I sent him to the mission hospital for a thorough examination. The report was clear: "Mingmatsering has four different types of worms— an unusual number to have at one time even in Nepal." He was given a powerful dose of medication and we saw little of him for two days. Then he returned, pale and shaky but already brighter of eye and with the old snap in his voice.

The Sherpas still accept supernatural reasons for much of their ill health, which is understandable when their lack of medical knowledge is considered. Angtemba, a shrewd and cynical individual of wide experience, once told us he had "carried a witch on his back for a week." Apparently he had been passing a village which harbored a notorious witch when he suddenly felt gripping pains on his back and sides. Do what he could, he was unable to dislodge his invisible visitor and only after a week of pain and frequent visits to the gompa was he able to gain his freedom. The other Sherpas, on hearing this tale, all nodded their heads in complete agreement and we soon had a spate of similar experiences. We asked if any action was ever taken against the witches. "Indeed no, sahib! Who would do harm to a witch? They are usually well-respected women in the village, and in any case if you killed a witch your soul would be tied to hers for a thousand lives!" Despite this acceptance of the supernatural in health matters, the Sherpas are now firm supporters of Western medicine and take full advantage of the treatment offered.

One of the most distressing features of life among the Sherpas is the high incidence of goiter and its related cretinism. Mountain people throughout the world have had goiter trouble, but it is easily overcome by the addition of iodine to the diet—easily, that is, if you have some means of ensuring that the iodine will be consumed regularly. The usual method is to iodize salt. But how can one add iodine to the rough rock salt brought over the border from Tibet? Even pills are effective only as long as the families will take them regularly over the years, and this you cannot expect the Sherpas to do without prompting and supervision. The incidence of cretinism is appallingly high; one of our leading Sherpas has four children, all of whom range from slightly subnormal to complete cretins. Many Sherpas have at least one cretin among their children. This is obviously one field in which drastic improvements could be made.

There is great need for a small hospital in the Khumbu region; one doctor and a dozen beds would probably be enough initially. It would then be possible for really sick people to come from the surrounding villages for treatment and stay in the hospital without depleting their small store of money in paying for accommodation. It would also be feasible to initiate and supervise health schemes such as the introduction of iodine, regular vaccinations and so on. I can think of no more satisfying task for a doctor than a couple of years spent working among these fine mountain people.

Chapter 7

THE MEMSAHIBS—"VERY FAST, VERY STRONG"

WE WERE to be joined in the final stages of the expedition by Louise Hillary, Ann Wilson, and Doreen Del Fium, a young geologist from Los Angeles, California. The fourth member of the party was Ralph Wyeth who, as the United Nations-appointed general manager of the Nepal Bank, had been a great help in Katmandu to my expedition. I planned to fly the four of them in by helicopter, and there was much exchanging of messages about this. The Nepalese Government had been given several large helicopters by the Russian Government, plus the loan of aircrew to fly them. The Nepalese had agreed that after an initial period they would pay the salaries and expenses of the flight. When they were unable to do this, the Russians recalled their airmen. Although the Foreign Office kept telling us that the crews were daily expected back, they never did return and the deposit I had paid on a flight to Khumjung was finally refunded. Perhaps it was just as well. We later learned that the Russian pilots were not keen to land this type of plane at 12,000 feet, and for safe operations at this altitude the aircraft would need 150 unimpeded yards for takeoff and landing—which isn't easy to find around Namche Bazar.

The only other helicopter in Nepal, the American Bell, was fully committed to other tasks, so I had to resort instead to having the girls flown in the small fixed-wing Pilatus Porter to Jiri—halfway to Khumjung—and letting them walk the rest of the way from there. In her diary Louise tells the story of this trip:

Louise Hillary's Impressions

"18th May.

I just can't believe that I am really sitting in the middle of the Himalayas! I am the revered 'bara memsahib' and I have ten faithful Sherpas at my beck and call. Today has been as close to heaven as any day in my life. We woke at 5:30 A.M. and had a quick breakfast. The weather was perfect and our gear was just the right amount for the Pilatus Porter. Father Moran arrived with a present for Kalden Sherpa and a tin of oysters for Ed. Our Swiss pilot was wonderfully careful and efficient. I didn't feel at all nervous during the flight. The mountains showed up huge and clear and our landing at Jiri was amazing. We had to approach the tiny 200-yard strip from below and sort of hop over a little mountain. It was a successful landing, but if I hadn't had faith in the pilot I would never have believed we could make it alive. As I write, it is pouring rain and a Sherpa ruffian is singing a song as he digs a ditch round my tent.

After landing we walked for three hours, mostly in hot sunshine, and arrived at the Khimti Khola to camp beside a rushing stream near a village. The 'bara memsahib' (as the Sherpas called me) had her tent erected and her air mattress and sleeping bag fixed mighty quickly—also shoes put out and all her valuables. Then the other tents went up more slowly. The Sherpas made tea for us, and then I had a good wash. We all sat around eating litchis (an Asiatic stone fruit) and listening to a cuckoo. When Lakpa asked me about dinner I gave assorted commands, but nearly got blinded by smoke in the Sherpas' abode when I went to check on progress.

I had a wonderful night's sleep and at 5 A.M. heard that heavenly early morning sound. 'Memsahib, cha.' I unzipped the tent and found a grinning Sherpa face waiting outside with tea and biscuits. Then followed the usual procedure of dressing and washing while all our stuff was packed. The Sherpas, all ten of them, are our great friends. There is 'Blue Pants,' who laughs all the time, and Jatzu, whom we call 'Samson' and who sings as he carries a fantastic load. Sen Tenzing is proving a good sirdar. We walked up a 2500-foot hill in the glorious early morning to find purple orchids and dainty white ones. The Sherpas entered into the fun of it and picked flowers for me and sang. 'Blue Pants' got very hot but staggered faithfully on behind. We all put flowers on top of the pass and yelled 'Soh soh soh.' Lakpa Tsering (Mingma's younger brother) wore Doreen's pretty raffia hat on which I had put a rhododendron. I took the big hill down to Chyangma Gompa slowly to give my knees a chance. Lakpa stuck to me like glue—he is determined to get me to his bara sahib in one piece. At Chyangma we bought 300 eggs for Ed.

Breakfast was a huge meal—it took two and a half hours —cereal, potato chips, omelet, tea twice, chapatties, litchis. After a perfect, happy day we camped down in the Likhu Khola.

20th May.

I had rather a hot night but felt refreshed after a cup of tea and a cold wash in the river. Then we started the biggest climb I have ever done—7000 feet up a mountain to the top of the Lamjura Banyang Pass at 12,000 feet. 'Samson' was in a bad temper. He thought he had too heavy a pack, so he didn't sing and life seemed rather sad. The new porters failed to appear and we wondered if our happy party was breaking up. Two thousand feet up 'Samson' started to sing and the first little white and yellow-throated orchids appeared. All was well. We saw pink orchids and wonderful deep valleys, all blue with distance, and trees covered with starry white orchids.

Halfway up the ridge we stopped at a teahouse for

rather long, as the Sherpas felt the need for a rest. It was
hard work staggering upwards through the cold clouds, but
there were masses of pink-and-white rhododendrons to take
one's mind off the steep track. We saw yellow primroses,
pink forget-me-nots and white buttercups. I sang all the
way down the other side of the mountain amongst rhododendrons, magnolias, and fir trees. We camped in a meadow
at 11,000 feet, where it was cold and windy. A large hairy
dzhum looked as though it would attack me, so I retreated
to the Sherpas for protection and they drove it off with
shrieks of laughter. We had a marvelous dinner of chicken-
and-rice curry and cauliflower. The tent shook all night under the fierce wind and I hardly slept.

21st May.

It was a windy and cold morning and the Sherpas were a
bit late with tea. I went wandering about with my head in
air to look at magnolias, then fell into a bog and emerged
wet and dirty. A young mother arrived with a baby boy who
had a very sore foot. I found my few medical things and
took the mother to the stream, then popped a barley sugar
in the child's mouth and started work. It looked like a burn
and was caked with filth. We ordered plenty of *garam pani*
and *sawun* (hot water and soap) and gave her some extra
dressings. Feeling like real doctors, we trooped down the
hill amongst the flowers and the crops and into the cozy,
prosperous village of Junbesi. Breakfast was in the gompa
courtyard, as it was now raining, and then we had more
medical problems. One was a nasty infected finger that we
hardly dared touch. Again we prescribed hot water and soap.

The walk round the great rolling grassy hills above Junbesi was a day in paradise. There were yellow perennials
and daisies and forget-me-nots. Down below two or three
thousand feet were sparkling rivers; above them lush terraces of barley, wheat and potatoes. Prosperous houses, all
freshly whitewashed, with solid wooden roofs and little

stone terraces, were clustered here and there. Above the high summer pastures were dark forests and then dazzlingly white, jagged peaks.

We crawled up to the pass at Taksindu, said our *Soh sohs* to the gods, and with Sen Tenzing's alcoholic breath blowing us downhill we soon arrived at Taksindu Gompa. The lamas didn't want us to camp there, even though Sen Tenzing said he would put the tents well out of the way. But the lamas still complained and were rather unpleasant so I got on my high horse and said we would camp elsewhere. Down we went through the forest in a thick mist, getting more tired every minute. We stumbled on until nearly dark. Kamin picked a whole lot of wild strawberries and gave them to us, which was very sweet of him. Our camp was damp and full of insects but soon a big fire was going and we crowded around it. The porters with our tents didn't turn up till after dark so there was some pandemonium. A couple of rough-looking local men appeared and stood eying my pack (with its 12,000 rupees in it). Lakpa stood his ground and looked fierce until at last they moved off.

22nd May.

I had a good night though it was cold. I slept till 5:30 as I had told our crew they could sleep in for an extra hour after yesterday's big effort. Mail runners from Khumjung woke me with a letter from Ed. We set off at 6:30 and dashed down the hill to have a gorgeous swim in the Dudh Kosi River. There we washed all our clothes and waited for the sun to dry them. The rushing river, the light-green trees, the white peaks above us were a joy. Pemba Jansi came along with a bunch of flowers for me. Nearly all the Sherpas have had a good bath, and Lakpa is all spruced up with clean hair and clean clothes.

After a breakfast of cereal, potato chips and fried chapatties we crossed the Dudh Kosi with trepidation on a rickety bough bridge with the foaming water lapping the bottom of it. Jatzu saw one of the old Sherpas looking a bit worried so dropped his load and carried the old man's for him. Even so the old chap prayed very hard to the gods as he crossed over. The hill up to Kharikhola proved to be a terrible pull, especially as we girls took the wrong path and Sen Tenzing had to run after us.

For dinner we had no meat of any kind so they made us a dish we called *Compote de Legumes Kharikhola*—beans, potato and cabbage with a mild chili gravy. During dinner we heard some strange groaning noises in the darkness and were terrified. Ralph went out to explore and found it was a sad cold Indian from the plains who was servant to an Indian Survey team camped nearby.

23rd May.

On waking, we hastened to the river to get cleaned up in anticipation for meeting our menfolk. I didn't feel too well but climbed the steep 2500-foot hill easily, considering everything. We stopped for breakfast in a sandfly-ridden place and I had only two spoonfuls of oatmeal, a cup of tea, and some medicine. At the end of the meal we heard wild yells above us and thought it was the men, so rushed up the path, answering loudly. To our chagrin we only met some Nepalese coolies singing happily as they came down the track. We felt like pricked balloons and didn't dare face our Sherpas, who obviously knew all the time that we had made a mistake. We puffed our way up the wretched hill and at last reached the top. We were only a short way down the other side when we saw two men climbing up the hill towards us. We were quite sure this time they were our party, so decided to ambush them. We leaped off the track but didn't have time to hide properly. It was Ed and Jim Wilson, deep in discussion. They walked past us even though we were so obvious—Ed was saying, 'And do you know the bloody so-and-so even tried to steal our peaches.'

We were fascinated and wanted to hear more, but instead let out a loud whoopee!—and I still haven't heard the end of the story."

Ceremonial Greeting

We had walked several days downvalley to meet the girls and it was good to see them pop up looking so fit and brown. We celebrated with a sumptuous repast of roast chicken, roast potatoes, onions and beans, followed by apricots and custard. The potatoes were new-season, freshly dug, and were absolutely delicious. At this lower altitude they were much in advance of the Khumjung potatoes, which were only now pushing their heads above surface.

We carried on up the Dudh Kosi Valley next day and it was something of a triumphal march with many people lining the track to see us pass—especially to look at the famous memsahibs, whose reputation of being "very fast and very strong" had gone on ahead of them. We breakfasted at Surkya and were visited by a sadly pock-marked boy—a smallpox victim who had been lucky enough to survive. Four others had died in this tiny village.

After breakfast we carried on until we were met by four of the senior citizens of the large village of Chaunrikharka. They held out garlands of flowers and a Tibetan pony covered in bright-colored rugs and with bells around his neck. We were all garlanded and then Louise was invited to ride the pony into the village half a mile away. The Sherpas had learned quickly that if you wanted to please someone you did honor to his wife.

Louise rode on ahead, having to stop every now and then to receive more flowers. Just below the village it was rough and steep, and on the slopes above the entire population of Chaunrikharka was waiting with more garlands to greet us. The saddle had been loosened by the rough track and chose this moment to give trouble. In slow motion it slid down the horse's side and Louise, bedecked with flowers, was precipitated in highly undignified fashion onto the ground. Unhurt and still cheerful, she was helped to her feet by the Sherpas. The girth was very firmly tightened, Louise clambered aboard once more and the triumphal procession continued.

In the center of the village a ceremonial arch had been built; here the elders of the village met us and presented us with scarves. Through the arch were about fifty school children, all with scarves and flowers and calling out *"Zindabar Sir Hillary"* over and over again. We were led to a special enclosure where benches were covered with bright Tibetan rugs. There were flowers and prayer flags and a wonderful gleaming copper heating arrangement underneath a large teapot. Tibetan tea was immediately served in dainty Chinese dishes and, so as not to offend, we drank all we could bear.

Finally came the purpose of the whole display—as purpose of course there was. The village wanted help with their school. The government made an annual grant of Rs 800 ($105), but this was proving totally inadequate. For two hours we listened to their stories. Most vociferous of all was the Nepalese schoolteacher. We decided to examine his case, for he was passionately declaiming that starvation was staring him in the face. It was impossible to get unprejudiced information from the teacher himself, but the headmen told us that he received all the Rs 800 together with the free supply by the village of a room, food and a boy to do his chores. In fact the teacher was being quite well treated according to local standards. The school itself had few books and no writing material and the learning was confined to intoning sentences behind the schoolmaster. We were saved from an even longer discourse by the approach of a heavy rain shower. We sheltered in the ramshackle building that served as a school and had practical experience of its inadequacy, for the water poured through the roof and the wind whistled in completely unchecked. I agreed to do what I could for the school, but said they would have to wait a year or so for any major assistance. At the end of the expedition I donated sufficient supplies of books, paper, pencils and slates etc. for a year's use.

Because the rain showed no signs of stopping, we carried on into it. Drenched and frozen, we arrived at the small village of Ghat and were met by another reception committee, less well organized but much fuller of chang than the first, and had to listen to a strong presentation of the virtues of Ghat rather than Chaunrikharka as the school site. Retaining my patience with difficulty—I am not at my agreeable best when listening to drunkards in the rain—I managed to close the meeting in something approaching harmony and continued upvalley. Fortunately the rain now ceased. We soon dried out under the vigorous effort of clambering up and down the steep, narrow path. We camped on a pleasant terrace beside the flooded Dudh Kosi and drifted off to sleep to the tune of glacial boulders grinding and bumping their way down towards the sea.

Our arrival at Khumjung can best be told by Louise.

Further Notes from Louise's Diary

"*25th May.*

We were all too excited to sleep very well, and anyway I think the altitude was affecting us a bit. We walked for two hours beside the roaring Dudh Kosi before stopping for breakfast. After a good meal we had to climb up and down on the steep sides of the gorge on wooden ladders. I didn't like this at all and the porters found it most trying. We crossed the river by a bridge in the bottom of the gorge and then climbed up a steep and exposed track onto the ridge above. Ann wasn't feeling at all well and Jim and Pembertarkay had to take turns carrying her up this fierce 3000 feet on their backs. We were met halfway up the hill by a reception committee led by Mingma and his wife, with the women all dressed up in the most glorious aprons and jewelry. Mrs. Chumbi was there also and the expedition liaison officer, K. C. Sahib, who presented us with flowers. Mingma's little boys were there in their best clothes—Ang Temba, 8, Ang Shita, 3, Yungjen, 1. On the west of the ridge was a table and cloth with flowers and a box of sweet cakes. We sat down on a glorious rug and Mrs. Chumbi and Mrs. Tsering gave us maize beer and rice beer, coffee and cocoa till we were nearly swamped. It was quite delightful. We then floated up to Namche between lovely blue irises and bright yellow flowers that were new to me.

At Namche village Karmatila invited us in for tea and potatoes and beer. It was all most jolly. It started to pour rain but we staggered upwards to Khumjung, where we had a terrific welcome. Desmond was there and all the village lined beside a triumphal arch. Tem Dorje, the teacher, presented me with a scarf and all the school children sang out 'Welcome, bara Memsahib.' The headmen of the village were a glorious array of old pirates. We moved en masse to the school building, which was arrayed in primulas and rhododendrons. The place was shining and it was a thrill to see it after having heard so much about it. We were offered coffee, tea, cocoa, chang, and rakshi by the gallon. Then the children sang to us most beautifully—they were so well trained, clean-faced and intelligent.

It was freezing cold and wet but after a time the sky cleared and we went walking up to gompa to see the new water supply where Murray Ellis and Phudorje were working, making large storage tanks. We saw Mike Gill and Phil Houghton's Surgery at the gompa—it was most comfortable. We had a good big dinner in the mess tent, which was freezing despite a little wood stove. However, we laughed so much that no one noticed the cold. Ralph Wyeth brought out the four royal photos we had brought to put in the schools. To our horror they were smashed to bits! As the poor smudged pictures were shown to us, we all stood up and K. C. sang the national anthem. Then we went through the prizes for the school sports, which was one of the funniest things I have ever done for we didn't have enough prizes and had to cut up various things. All night I kept laughing about it, as I found the altitude made it difficult to sleep."

Sports Day for the Three Schools

The day following the party's arrival was an important one at Khumjung, for we were organizing the first annual school sports. Children came from Pangboche School and even from Thami. The weather looked grim to start with but gradually improved. Murray made a loud hailer [megaphone] out of some aluminum sheeting and one of the Sherpas paraded outside the village and called the people to come to the sports. By 9:30 A.M. they were streaming in by the hundreds—and what a sight it was! There were old men and women, mostly toothless, spinning their prayer wheels and counting their beads; then handsome, wealthy middle-aged people dressed magnificently in gold, silver and turquoise jewelry; young men mostly in smart expedition clothing and expensive-looking continental boots; and pretty girls with rosy, rounded cheeks, long, shining black plaits and sparkling eyes. There were hoards of children of every size and shape, some well clad and clean, some in torn and grubby clothing, but all bubbling over with anticipation. There must have been at least 600 people altogether and still they kept coming.

Desmond had organized a complicated program using a great deal of ingenuity. (I discovered later that he had been in charge of sports and entertainments for his Gurkha regiment.) There were thirty-two races altogether, ranging from potato races for the girls to an obstacle race, specially designed by Desmond, in which the boys at the starter's whistle had to pull on their Tibetan boots, climb over a jungle gym, run along a pole above the ground, jump over a fence, wriggle through a suspended hoop, and crawl through long tunnels of bamboo matting before dashing madly for the finishing line. The audience nearly split with laughter watching the antics of their children. For the young ones there was a race to eat a chapatty suspended from a string and liberally plastered with sticky honey—and I have rarely seen such determination or such sticky faces.

Before the sports we gathered around the flagpole in front of the flower-festooned school and Mr. Tem Dorje, the headmaster, explained to the throng about Nepal, the Nepalese flag and the national anthem. Then we stood at attention while the flag was raised and the children sang the national anthem. I tried to take every opportunity of emphasizing to the Sherpas their identity with Nepal to counteract to some extent the subtle propaganda being spread from Tibet.

For the adults there were the shot-put and the 100-yard sprint, both won by Jim Wilson with Pembertarkay coming a close second. In the sprint Khuncha managed to come third even after he'd taken time off during the course of the race to place his hat carefully on the sideline. There was much barracking in the tugs of war. First Phorche village pulled against Khumjung. The wealthy farmers of Khumjung were a tough mob in their bakhus, pigtails, and gold and turquoise earrings; the Phorche team were mostly burly Sherpa climbers like Siku, Pembertarkay and Sen Tenzing. They pulled until they were black in the face; no one would give in, until finally the Khumjung men were dragged relentlessly over the line.

Phudorje was the strongest man in the Khunde team, and pulled his side to victory in the most ferocious display of brute strength you could imagine, even taking time off to spit on his hands to keep his grip good. In fact Khunde came out the final winner and Sirdar Mingmatsering (whose village this was) had difficulty in preventing a far from impartial grin of pleasure from sweeping over his countenance.

Because the Sherpas appeared tired after their efforts, and reassured by the knowledge that we weighed at least 20 pounds extra per man, I thought it safe to challenge them to a representative fixture with the sahibs. Our seven-man heavyweight team started with a fine flourish but ended up by being dragged on its knees in the dirt, and although one disgruntled member claimed that an extra half-dozen Sherpas had leaped out from the crowd onto the local end of the rope, we magnanimously conceded defeat and went off to patch up our rope-burned hands and battered knees.

The last item of the day was a Sherpa climbing race up the rough ground and steep rocks across from the school. Down two great erratic boulders we had suspended rope ladders, and in other places we put fixed ropes. Teams of two took part. We made sure that the teams were evenly balanced. It was a fascinating race to watch, for the experienced Sherpas were so much better and faster than the young and inexperienced ones and yet didn't seem to be rushing it anywhere near as much. The veteran Angtemba got his young partner around the course in very good time to take first place.

By now it had started to rain, but all the onlookers stayed while Louise handed out the prizes from the table in front of the official stand, a gaily decorated Tibetan tent specially hired for the occasion by Desmond. Everyone then drifted home through the gloom and rain to the universally expressed view of both Sherpas and expedition members that it had been a rousingly successful day.

Here is the day's program, with the various prizes made up of items either brought in by Louise or the results of frantic searchings through their luggage by expedition members. We were so short of prizes that in a number of cases large gifts were divided in half and presented to two children.

PROGRAM

Prizes

1. Flag hoisting and national song
2. Shot-put (boys) — Ball-point pen
3. 75-yard sprint (intermediate) — 3 crayons and Louise's notebook
4. 3-legged race (junior) — Half a drawing set
5. Girls' potato race — Hair clips
6. 50-yard sprint (junior boys) — Magic slate
7. 100-yard sprint (senior boys) — Bhanu's ball-point pen
8. Tug of war (Khumjung v. Phorche)
9. 100-yard sprint (senior boys) — My KLM key ring
10. Kangaroo race (girls) — 3 crayons and a book
11. Girls' needle-and-thread race — Hair clips
12. Shot-put (men) — 10 rupees
13. 3-legged race (intermediate) — Black pencils
14. Kangaroo race (infants) — Modeling clay
15. 75-yard sprint (intermediate boys) — Ball-point pen
16. Tug of war (Khunde v. Namche)
17. Women's race — Handkerchief and Louise's soap
18. Broad jump (senior boys) — Modeling clay
19. 3-legged race (infants) — Half a drawing set
20. Kangaroo race (senior boys) — Tom's penknife
21. 100-yard sprint (open to all) — Murray's silk scarf
22. Chapatty-and-honey race — Magic slate

Prizes

23. Broad jump   Jim's ball-point pen
    (intermediate boys)
24. Kangaroo race (junior boys)   3 crayons and a book
25. Tug of war final   10 rupees per man
    (Khunde v. Phorche)
26. Kangaroo race   Ball-point pen
    (intermediate boys)
27. 3-legged race (senior boys)   Half a drawing set
28. Tug of war
    (sahibs v. the rest)
29. Obstacle race (juniors)   Coloring set
30. Obstacle race   Coloring set
    (intermediate)
31. Obstacle race (seniors)   Ball-point pen
32. Sherpa climbing race   15 rupees per man

Chapter 8

SCHOOLHOUSE ON THE TIBETAN BORDER

My MEMORIES of the village of Thami had not been happy ones. In 1951 and 1952 I had occasionally spent a night there on the way up the valley to the Tesi Lapcha Pass or Cho Oyu and had gained an impression of a dour, unsmiling people and a lack of enthusiasm for dealings of any sort with foreigners. In a village renowned for its potatoes we had been unable to buy a single meal, and felt this was all part of the cold-shoulder policy. Although time had mellowed my feelings, Thami had never become one of my favorite villages. Even its location has less appeal. The peaks surrounding are just as grand but the valley itself gives an impression of dry barrenness. The various widely spread groups of houses making up the village squat in rather unlovely fashion on flattish ledges high above the river. And the wind blows unceasingly. To the north the valley climbs in a jumble of moraine and dry pastures to a notch in the Himalayan range, the Nangpa La Pass which leads to Tibet. Although over 19,000 feet high this pass is not a difficult one, and men and yaks cross over its smooth glaciers with little difficulty in the summer months. Only a few miles away in Tibet is the town of Tingri. Our Sherpas told us of large encampments of Chinese soldiers and a forest of radio-communication aerials there.

In November 1960 we had crossed from the Rolwaling Valley over to Thami and found the area transformed. Camped about the village on every available space were thousands of Tibetan refugees. Their animals had been driven over the border with them but were dying from lack of grazing. In a desperate effort to save such a valuable source of food, the Tibetans were slaughtering the animals and drying the meat for future use. The main refugee encampment was an astonishing sight: hundreds of half-domed tents of varying sizes and quality, ranging from the black homespun hovel of the poorer man to more orthodox structures of white canvas magnificently decorated with leaping antelopes. Between all the tents lines had been strung, and on these thousand upon thousand of pieces of meat were drying in the moistureless air.

The refugees at this stage were far from destitute. We were entertained in the tent of the senior headman and were served out of gold- and silver-embossed bowls. But already the Tibetans were having to sell off their prized possessions, and as they were now completely unproductive, this could have only one inevitable consequence. These Tibetans were, in general, incredibly dirty. The Sherpas in their villages have not been renowned for frequent ablutions—the temperature and the shortage of fuel and even water are against it—but the black, dirt-encrusted hands, faces and feet of the Tibetans showed they rarely if ever washed themselves. Presumably on the arid dusty Tibetan plateau the peasant people (as these were) accept the soot and grime of smoky yak-dung fires as the normal and natural condition. Even among the Sherpas we found the belief of a distinct therapeutic effect in smoke. Some oldsters went so far as to forecast an increase in bodily ailments if the smoke in their homes were chimneyed out through the roof in effete Western fashion.

By 1963 most of the Tibetan tents had gone from the Thami fields. With their food and most of their finances exhausted, the Tibetans were drifting downvalley to kindlier climates and more possibilities of trading or begging. But by no means all the Tibetans had left the area. A few still lived in their simple tents. Many had purchased or rented

Sherpa homes and moved into them. This was made possible by the fact that most Sherpa families possessed several houses in different locations—a house with each potato area, a house in each yak grazing pasture and so on. Thami was now the largest concentration of people in the area, at least half of whom were Tibetans.

To the casual eye there isn't too much difference between Sherpas and Tibetans. The Sherpas are, of course, of Tibetan origin; their customs and dress are basically Tibetan, and their religious loyalty has always been to the Dalai Lama and the great monasteries of Tibet. Although the Tibetan monasteries have been destroyed by the Chinese, the Sherpa monasteries still carry on as before with many refugee Tibetan lamas in residence. The Sherpa language is a dialect of Tibetan, but it has sufficient individuality for most Tibetans not to understand it. This is rarely a problem, because most Sherpas speak Tibetan. In a group of Sherpas and Tibetans it is usually not difficult to separate them. Apart from minor differences in dress, the Tibetans are a taller race and have a certain fierce look about them that contrasts strongly with the quieter and more peaceful mien of the average Sherpa.

By virtue of its location near the Nangpa La Pass, Thami has close contact with Tibet and is a hotbed of underground activity. The Nepalese checkpost officer at Namche Bazar gave as his opinion that at least fifty per cent of the remaining Tibetans in Thami were to some degree controlled or paid by the Chinese. It was quite clear that a school would be a stabilizing factor in this community, and I was therefore keen to act on the petition from the village elders to "make our children like Khumjung."

Desmond, Murray and I visited Thami early in April for our first discussions with the village. We were met by the village elders and conducted to the proposed site. It was an excellent position, a gently sloping piece of common land with ample room for a playing field and superb views

of Tamserku and Kangtega. Towards the head of the valley
we could see the deep notch of the Nangpa La and the pale-
blue sky of Tibet. The village was full of enthusiasm and under Mingmatsering's guidance already had large quantities
of rock and timber stacked around the site.

The smallpox epidemic was still raging in this area. Next
morning we vaccinated at least 200 people before breakfast.
Then we had our official meeting with the village elders.
They were an impressive group and, dressed in their Tibetan finery, showed signs of considerable wealth. One of
the more important families were the parents of Tenzing
Norgay's new wife, and a handsome group they were. Tenzing, my Everest companion, had sent a note asking them to
help me all they could and they were giving an eager response. Thami has always claimed to be the original home
of Tenzing and he certainly spent some time there when he
was a young boy. But the older Sherpas say that Tenzing
was actually born in Tibet and came in over the Nangpa
La, that in fact he is technically more Tibetan than Sherpa.
Be this as it may, Tenzing certainly regards himself as a true
Sherpa—and he is, of course, the most famous of them all.

We spent several hours at the school site marking out its
dimensions so that the villagers could get on with the building of the rock walls. We found it difficult to convey our
meaning. To tell the construction team of three stonemasons
and a young lama that we wanted a building 40×20 feet
with 8-foot walls meant nothing, for they were not familiar
with the foot as a unit of measurement. Murray and Desmond drew clever sketches of the school and we gave the
men several 5-foot rules and explained their use, but we
departed from Thami with the uneasy feeling that little had
been understood.

SLOW—*School Ahead*

When I made a quick return visit twelve days later I was pleasantly surprised at the progress. Three stout rock walls stood firmly against the strong Tibetan wind and their horizontal dimensions were within a few inches of our requests.

"You can start building tomorrow, sahib," stated the senior rock mason.

Great was his chagrin when I measured things up and pointed out that the walls were still eighteen inches too low. However, cheerfulness soon prevailed and they promised to complete the job in the next few days. Quite a lot of timber had been collected but this was proving an arduous and difficult job. Far down in the gorge of the Bhote River was a pine forest clinging to the precipitous sides. Trees there were being felled and pitsawn into size. Then the wet timber was being carried by groups of men up to the school. It took the villagers at least four hours to do a round trip with a load, and as this was a voluntary village effort it had to be worked in with all their other, ordinary tasks. Despite the assurances of the Thami headman that all the timber would be on the site in ten days, I could see considerable delays ahead of us.

Over the next two weeks various reports came in from Thami indicating that progress was less than good. These were the initial signs of the subtle but growing opposition to the school which was being developed by a communist element in the village—an opposition that was always indirect and always hard to track down. Desmond agreed to go up to Thami and supervise the activity there. His arrival drove the opposition temporarily underground and satisfactory progress was made with completing the rock work, excavating the site, and accumulating the timber.

On May 14 Murray took a building team up the valley to

45. With adjustment here and there, the Thami School walls go up on the gently sloping land

46. Jim Wilson helping to complete roof at Thami

47. With the Nepalese flag raised against a panorama of Tamserku and Kangtega, the national anthem marks opening ceremonies

48. Skeleton of Thami School

49. Foundation stone

50. Young scholars practice lines of Nepali

51. Following the example at school exercises

52. The eight good-luck signs of Buddhism join a subtle blend of Sherpa, Tibetan and Western architecture

complete the job. Several days later I walked up to join them along a path lined with flowering rhododendrons, irises and primulas. I was most impressed with the progress. The roof structure was already in place, and the corrugated sheets were being nailed on. We had decided to use even more Sherpa architectural features in this building and they were already taking form. Under the eaves were the decorative cornices called locally the *langdy pangdy*. The windows were an open lattice of vertical and horizontal wooden slats, but with glass behind them to keep out the usual Sherpa drafts. Desmond was in excellent humor and regaled us with the gossip he had accumulated during his long stay in Thami—and his forebodings about the communist activity.

As we lunched at 1:30 P.M., heavy clouds rolled up the valley and we were deluged with rain. We sheltered in Desmond's tent for a couple of hours and the time passed quickly as we talked over forthcoming plans. The rain stopped by 4 P.M. and I set off back to Khumjung accompanied by two Sherpas. As we progressed down the path I was amazed to see that what had been rain at Thami had been snow farther down the valley. Below Namche Bazar the blanket of snow went all the way down to the river at 10,000 feet, a most unseasonable sight. We trudged up to Khumjung in three inches of wet, heavy snow. Our camp was in a sorry state—tents drooping under heavy loads of wet snow, pools of water everywhere and consequent mud and slush. My thought turned to the rock face on Taweche and I could imagine the wet snow avalanches that must be pouring off it and was very glad that we were clear of the mountain.

In the evening the skies cleared while the faces of our Sherpas got longer and longer. "Our crops will be ruined, sahib, if we get a heavy frost," Mingmatsering said. "The fields are just sprouting and this is the worst possible time."

By midnight the snow was crisp under a light frost. It

took a morning of warm sun to melt the snow off the fields
and reveal the tender sprouts brown and withered. Little
groups of Sherpas wandered disconsolately around their
fields and shook their heads in sorrow—it would be a complete crop failure, they said. By evening a slightly more
cheeful note was prevailing. The village council had met
and examined the situation. They agreed that the crop was
severely affected but certainly not destroyed. Still, the village would have to face another year of poor crops.

That 1962 had been itself a poor year had soon become
apparent to our expedition. Not only did we have difficulty
in buying ample supplies of potatoes, but there was also a
shortage of the potent spirit, rakshi. The Sherpas distill the
rakshi from potatoes and it is drunk on all important occasions (and on unimportant ones as well). We had noted
how infrequently the dirty rakshi bottle had made its appearance and had been entertained almost exclusively on
the local chang (beer) which is made out of millet. As I
much preferred the chang to the raw rakshi I had not re-
gretted this omission, but realized it indicated a considerable potato shortage among the Sherpas.

"It will be another year without rakshi for our village,"
said Mingmatsering, "and some people may have to go out
and get work." I asked him what happened when there was
a succession of bad crops.

"One bad crop is not too difficult. We stay on our land
and use up our surplus food, but tighten our belts a little.
Two bad crops are not so good. What small store of money
we may have is used to buy food, and any family treasures
may be sold. Those who have nothing must go downvalley
and find work. But three bad years are too much. Many
Sherpas have to take their families downvalley to warmer
and easier conditions and find work or subsist somehow.
Some may even die.

"Things have been better, sahib, since we started working for mountaineering expeditions. This has brought a

store of money into the villages and most of us have put some of this aside for the tough years."

It is often hard for us to realize how what we would regard as a tiny sum in cash can tide a village over an emergency. In 1962 Pangboche village had a complete failure in its potato crop. "How did you manage to survive the year?" I asked. "Each family had worked on your airfield in the Mingbo Valley, sahib," I was told, "and had put a store of money aside. This helped us through until the next crop." I paid out Rs 8000 for labor on the Mingbo airstrip in 1961—all to Pangboche people—and this would have averaged about Rs 135 ($18) per family. This modest sum, used wisely by the villagers, had served to keep them from starvation.

The Secret of Genuine Help

I am firmly convinced that one of the finest ways of helping an undeveloped community is to give the opportunity for worth-while and profitable employment. Free handouts are rarely successful. Too often the money or goods go into the hands of the wealthy traders who need it least. But by creating jobs for the community, the money goes into the individual homes where it does the most good (and the traders benefit as well). Perhaps most important of all, if a man devotes his strength and skill to some worth-while task he not only feels he has earned the money honestly but he retains his pride and his independence in the process.

By May 20 Thami School was almost completed, and now that the memsahibs had arrived we could make definite plans for the opening ceremony. Pupils had been signed on some two weeks before, and the two schoolmasters, Phutsering and Kalden, had been conducting classes out in the open fields. Once again the head lama of Thyangboche had agreed to be present at this ceremony—agreed with enthusiasm, for Thami was his home village, where he had been discovered as a reincarnate child and taken off for monastery training in Tibet. He also confessed to us his concern at some of the activities in Thami. "Too many men have too much money," he said. "It doesn't come from yaks or potatoes. It can only come from over the border."

The morning of May 27 was a busy one at Khumjung as we started getting organized for the Thami School opening. At 12 A.M. the head lama's secretary arrived from Thyangboche to say that the head lama was approaching our camp en route to Thami. We dashed madly around making preparations, laying down our best carpet and putting a comfortable chair on it. He strode into camp with a welcoming smile and I led him to the place of honor we had prepared. What an interesting personality he was! Very Mongolian in appearance, intelligent and restless yet extremely dignified, he had a wicked sparkle in his eye. We served up a fine lunch of tomato soup, then boiled new potatoes, butter, salt and ground chili peppers. After lunch a pony covered in a fine carpet and complete with bells was led up, whereupon the head lama departed on the final stage of his trip.

Soon after we set out as well. We walked down the hill to Namche Bazar to see the American Everest Expedition, which was camped there after its great triumphs on the mountain. Norman Dyhrenfurth, the leader, greeted us warmly. It was most enjoyable to meet and talk with the fine men of his team. They were a battered and scarred group after their long spell at high altitudes, and I found it most interesting to compare notes after a gap of ten years. The successful ascent of the West Ridge of Everest by Willi Unsoeld and Tom Hornbein will long remain one of the really spectacular feats of mountaineering.

We carried on to Thami and had a pleasant three-hour walk while Louise exclaimed over the irises and clematis, the yellow and white rhododendrons, the primulas and the forget-me-nots. At Thami there were a welcoming arch and an official group to greet us with ceremonial scarves, chang, rakshi and hot tea. Despite the cold temperatures and strong wind a considerable crowd had gathered, and obviously excitement was building up for the various ceremonies on the next day. The head lama was staying in the largest house in the village, and to keep away the curious, a large and ferocious mastiff dog had been let loose in the bottom story. We had with us two Nepalese porters who were familiar with neither Sherpa customs nor mastiffs. In looking for a protected place to spend the night, it was their bad luck to open the door of the house containing the head lama. Only one of the Nepalese got inside the door before the mastiff leaped out of the darkness and clamped his teeth firmly shut on the man's calf. With a shriek of mortal agony he leaped in the air and managed to shake the dog loose. As he shot out the door he received a parting nip in the seat of his pants. The two men, pale and trembling, soon arrived at our camp for medical attention. Phil Houghton patched up the injured man and then put him to bed in a tent. The Sherpas regarded it all as something of a joke, but it certainly increased our respect for any mastiff. We crouched around a meager fire until 9 P.M. and then escaped into the warmth of our sleeping bags.

Dedication of Thami School

In her diary Louise describes the next two days:

"*28th May.*

We tried to sleep in but Desmond woke us with the news that the H. L. [head lama] was going up the hill to the Thami Gompa and that it would be worth our going to see the sights. As we struggled up the hill at 7 A.M. the clouds disappeared and we had blue sky above us with towering

white peaks all around—except up to the Nangpa La, which
was rolling and barren and defiant. The gompa clings to the
mountainside, and there is a most impressive view downvalley to Kangtega. We crept inside and saw the H. L. sitting cross-legged in his high seat. Below him sat the lamas
in two rows intoning their prayers—they did one that had a
fine melody but it was too smoky and dark for me to write
down the tune. We were all served Tibetan tea (ugh!) and
the H. L. graciously waved to us. After a while we heard
that the H. L. would be there until ten o'clock and would
be breakfasting in the gompa so we romped down the hill
to camp, picking flowers on the way. We had breakfast in
brilliant sunshine and then climbed up to the gompa again
and watched the end of the service when the H. L. was
blessing everyone. We were put on a fuss and were served
candy and tea—this time ordinary Indian tea and milk,
thank goodness. Finally Ed made a present of some money
to the gompa and the H. L. led us outside.

A local lama conducted us formally through the courtyard with a prayer flag in one hand and burning incense
in the other, but when we were clear of the gompa grounds
he let the H. L. lead the procession down to the school. Ed,
Desmond and the H. L. walked hand in hand, as it is the
done thing to support an important reincarnate. The clouds
were soft and fluffy, the sky blue, the river sparkling and
the world full of laughter. We hurried after H. L., who
moves fast, his flying magenta robes revealing glimpses of a
brilliant yellow brocade shirt. Every so often one of the
faithful would come up and received his blessing. We
walked down below the school and along past a great *mani*
wall and chorten to give us good luck. At the gate of the
school we were met by a large crowd and there was much
giving of scarves. Inside the school courtyard the H. L. sat
on a raised seat cross-legged with bright Tibetan rugs
around. The senior dignitaries sat on these. First of all the
H. L. said some prayers, then as the villagers and school

children trooped before him and gave offerings of maize, rice, etc., he blessed them. It was very like an Anglican Communion. First we each had blessed tea poured in our hand. We drank it and wiped the remains on our forehead. Then we walked bareheaded up to the lama and bowed our heads, which he touched with a sacred symbol. Then we were given a little ball of tsampa by a priest, a teaspoon of chang and a little white ribbon for round our necks. I suppose about 550 people went through.

Kalden Sherpa had a terrific struggle with his conscience. He was the young boy Ed had taken to Katmandu and put into the Jesuit school there. He had returned as junior teacher at Thami and was finding things rather difficult, as he now regarded himself as a Christian (having perhaps been more impressed with the material wealth of the West than its philosophy). At first he stood back and wouldn't go through and be blessed by the H. L. I think he watched in some astonishment as all of us went through in turn, even Ed. Jim Wilson, who is an ordained minister of the Presbyterian Church, was well in the lead. As he said, the blessing of a good man was worth having, whatever his religion. Finally, much to our relief, Kalden gave in and was blessed in his turn. No one seemed to take the slightest notice of all this, but I'm sure that it wasn't missed by anyone.

The Khumjung school children came round the hill halfway through the ceremony, singing songs in the crisp air. After the blessings I raised the flag and the school children sang the Nepal national anthem. Dressed in my new silk Bhutanese mandarin-collared shirt that I bought from a trader at breakfast time, I stood to attention with our liaison officer. Then Ed made a speech which Desmond translated and we all sat at the H. L.'s feet on glorious bright rugs— cross-legged of course, except for Ed whose legs are too long. The H. L. gave a good, forceful speech and he and I together cut the ribbon at the door of the schoolhouse.

The architecture of the schoolhouse is quite brilliant. It

would get an award anywhere in the world as a perfect blend of Sherpa, Tibetan, and Western. The roof is aluminum, the three walls stone and mud plaster, and the floor is rough-sawn planks. In the roof are three plastic roofing panels for lighting. The front wall is made of wood with small Sherpa-type window frames—but glass instead of rice paper. The beams holding up the roof come out under the eaves in traditional *langdy pangdy* pattern. Desmond painted the front wall bright traditional red and the *langdy pangdy* red and green. The bottom panel of the wall was painted with the eight lucky signs of the Bhuddist religion —the two fish, conch shell, wheel of life, etc.—all most beautifully done.

The ceremony took about four hours, and then we struggled out of the crowd and had the H. L. and staff for a simple lunch of soup and boiled potatoes. Not even butter was left. The crowd was a magnificent sight, all dressed in dashing bakhus and fur caps and with bright brocade shirts and knee-length boots. The women had striped aprons and wore gold and silver and turquoise jewelry. Everywhere were rosy-cheeked girls with white teeth and little boys with impish grins. 'Namaste salaam,' they all cried or, as they say it 'Namasaste.'

The afternoon became cold and windy with various crises. First there was smallpox. A little boy attending the school had just got over it and a deputation came to Ed asking that the child be kept away from school. A crowd gathered in the schoolmaster's ramshackle house (how the flooring kept intact I do not know), voices were raised higher and higher until suddenly I saw Ed reach out and grab a nasty-looking villain by the shoulder and shake him violently. It became more dramatic! The floor shuddered! But thank goodness this wild behavior made the throng more reasonable. Evidently this villain had threatened the schoolmaster with a beating if he admitted the boy, and Ed wrathfully told him that if there was going to be a beating he'd be on the receiving end of it. It all ended happily when Ed diplomatically said that the two doctors would examine the boy again, even though we knew he was well past the infectious stage.

Next we walked back to camp and met another deputation that wanted special payment for timber. They demanded 160 rupees, but after two hours of haggling in the freezing wind everybody was very happy with twenty rupees. By this time it was 4:30 P.M. and bitter. Ed looked cold and worn, whereas I had been sheltering for some time in Desmond's luxurious tent.

Oh what a long and puffy walk it was back to Khumjung! We had had little solid food and a most exciting, long day. Every step was an effort. I found myself almost crawling my way home. Luckily I remembered the last block of chocolate we possessed was in my pack, so I waited for Lakpa and he found it for me. We returned to Khumjung at 7 P.M. and sat down to a fine yak stew and then dahi and tsampa and sugar.

Ten Years

29th May.

A surprise day! We woke after a good sleep. Ed got up at 6 A.M. after our tea and left me to luxuriate in our big double bag, which was a relief as I had lain most of the night on a bag of cement. Our tent is the expedition storehouse and it's just horribly chaotic and there's never any privacy for a minute. At 7 A.M. Lakpa brought me my hot water and I washed and Ed and I gave him a pile of dirty clothes. For breakfast there was only cereal and potatoes. We had run out of flour. By midmorning we were so hungry that we raided Ed's stores of biscuits. Mingma put out a big camping table for me in the sun, I made Ed tell me all the letters he needed done, and I got to work on the creaking typewriter, surrounded by an admiring audience. I sat on a chair, two sleeping bags and a gorgeous Tibetan carpet square Angtemba had given Ed. I hadn't been writing for long when two of the usual hawkers came by with a carpet to sell. In a bored manner I asked them to unroll their wares and continued typing. Then I looked up and gave a yell to Ed—it was a pair of wildly colorful dragon rugs. Just exactly what I had been hunting for. They asked Rs 400 and I offered 300. In the end we got them for Rs 330 ($44).

A little later those two Everest veterans Annullu and Dawa Tenzing appeared and seemed most noncommittal about why they had arrived. Then Ed got hungry and searched out an almond cake the cook had made a few days before. Ed cut out a hunk, then said it was so awful that he threw it away. Mingma appeared from nowhere and quietly fielded it. Ed and I continued on with our work until the H. L.'s secretary appeared and stood around vaguely. After some time the H. L. arrived with his retinue and a very auspicious present for Ed. Luckily we had spread out our rugs for him and so the scene was set. In a beautifully woven Bhutanese basket he had some special rare Tibetan delicacy—a root called *tambo*—given only to the highest lamas and most special people. The basket was for me. He presented Ed and me and Mingma with scarves. Then we sat waiting for Desmond, who seemed to have been held up, for some time. At last he appeared complete with a partly mauled but now chocolate-iced almond cake with a huge flag on top and a note saying 'Many happy ten years of mountains.' The only person who was surprised was Ed, who had forgotten it was May 29. Annullu, Dawa Tenzing and Desmond and the H. L. and secretary and all the expedition then had a heartwarming Everest anniversary. Mingma stood up and made a speech in English and Dawa Tenzing made one and even Annullu—dear old Annullu—said a few words. Then they brought forth a bottle of rum.

The H. L. drank a sip and blessed it then we had a toast and all the Sherpas had a sip as well.

It started to rain so we had lunch in the mess tent—soup, potatoes and chilies as always. The H. L. was full of fun and Ed gave him a Sears Roebuck Thermos set. After lunch we took the H. L.—or should I say, the H. L. marched us relentlessly and swiftly up for a Khumjung water-supply inspection and also to the gompa, where the boys have their Surgery. Annullu and Dawa Tenzing got very excited about it all and Annullu was full of plans for future developments in Khumjung.

During the afternoon it became cold and wet and we were forced to call for umbrellas in the mess tent because of the drips. After Ed and Mingma had done much work on the Kunde water supply, they had some good beer at Mingma's house and then we all had roast yak and roast potatoes, dhal and rice, followed by 'delicious Indian apricots' which are terrible and 'delicious Indian custard,' ditto.

After dinner K. C., our liaison officer, who is a famous Nepalese poet, sang us a song in honor of Ed's ascent of Everest. He was dressed in his best Nepalese clothes and looked marvelous. The song was delightful and was wickedly interpreted stanza by stanza by Desmond. I liked the bit that went 'Sir Johna Hunta' and also how when Ed got to the summit he was free to go up or down whichever he chose. It was quite a battle controlling one's fits of giggles, as K. C.'s voice was rather wavery and it went on for fifteen minutes and was terribly serious.

Never has there been a more delightful Everest anniversary."

Chapter 9

RACE AGAINST THE MONSOON

KANGTEGA, 22,340 feet, is another of the inner circle of immense peaks surrounding the Khumbu. Compared with the outlying giants along the Tibetan border, these mountains are small; yet they dominate the villages and lower valleys, and it is a popular comment to describe their menacing rock walls and hanging ice as near or beyond the bounds of possibility. To the east the incomparable Ama Dablam soars skyward, one of the most breathtakingly lovely of all mountains. In March 1961 four members of my expedition made the first ascent of this peak (Mike Gill was one of the party). Above Pangboche stands Taweche, on which we had just been rebuffed. Chunky and rugged, it has the deceptive appearance of being the easiest of the four, although in Mike Gill's opinion it had proved more difficult than Ama Dablam. And then there is Kangtega, an array of grim black precipices rising close behind Thyangboche Monastery and overhung by a fringe of breaking ice cliffs. By contrast the summit itself is a lovely snow plateau rising to a pair of twin peaks separated by a snow saddle—hence the name: *Kang* is Tibetan for snow, *tega*, a saddle. The last of the four is Tamserku, perhaps the least photogenic and hence the least well known, but we know by now that it is also unequivocably the most difficult.

Mike Gill played as important a part on Kangtega as he did on Taweche. A brilliant climber on both ice and rock, he was undoubtedly the best acclimatized of our party and I will leave it to him to relate the story of Kangtega.

Kangtega
(BY MIKE GILL)

The Kangtega party set off on May 29—exactly the tenth anniversary of the first ascent of Everest. It was the only thing about our departure that could be termed even remotely auspicious, for the monsoon seemed to have broken in earnest, time was running short and it was a long, long way to the foot of the mountain.

Norman Dyhrenfurth, leader of the American Everest Expedition, had written that in his opinion Taweche should "go" but that on Kangtega he couldn't see even a suggestion of a possible route. But we held one trump card we were keeping quiet about; on the 1960–61 expedition we had caught glimpses of the final thousand feet of the hidden southern aspect of the peak; surprisingly it looked no more than a long snow slope steep, but nevertheless all snow. It was enough to encourage Dr. Jim Milledge to spend ten days walking round to the Inukhu Valley for a closer view at the lower slopes; and the report of only a single, relatively easy icefall guarding the mountain added to the picture of an easy southern approach.

This was the situation when Ed Hillary sought permission to attempt Kangtega, and during the expedition we were able to add confirmatory evidence from yet another viewpoint. While Phil Houghton was establishing that there was no possible route from the Monjo tributary of the Dudh Kosi, I made the first ascent of a minor, 19,800-foot peak on the Mingbo–Inukhu divide. There before me lay the route; there was Milledge's icefall leading to a long, gently rising glacier; there were the easy upper slopes; only a thousand feet of the middle section lay hidden behind a subsidiary ridge. Behind the awe-inspiring Khumbu façade of impossible precipice and hanging ice, the southern door lay open and waiting for us.

Three Days to the Impossible

It would have been easy but for the time factor. Given a month of good spring weather, all the sahibs could have reached the summit, half the Sherpas and maybe even a wife or two. But the Thami school had to be built and ceremoniously opened, there were wives to be welcomed and entertained, there was the Khumbu Sports Day . . . and so it was the end of May when the party started on its belated attempt with the first monsoon rains already drenching the lower valleys. With supreme optimism a schedule was worked out: five days from Khumjung to Base Camp at the foot of the icefall, one day forcing a route up the icefall, one day carrying in Camp I to 21,000; and the eighth day would be for the summit. It seemed fatuous allotting three days to climb a mountain that had often enough been declared impossible, but at least it was something to aim for.

The party was made up of about fifteen coolies with a minimal number of cretins and cripples, our top five high-altitude Sherpas led by Angtemba, and four sahibs: Dornan, Wilson and I were fit and acclimatized from our efforts on Taweche, and Frost seemed to have largely recovered from his debilitating bout of glandular fever and subsequent lack of acclimatization. The march to Base Camp was a long one, for although the summit was a mere five miles from Khumjung on the map, the route from the south could be approached only by a long detour down to Lukhla in the lower Dudh Kosi, and over a 16,000-foot yak pass into the Inukhu Valley. It was an area about which our Sherpas could give almost no information, least of all its name. As with a good many other names lifted from the Indian Survey map, the word Inukhu was met with blank incomprehension.

Setting off down the Dudh Kosi, we seemed to be traveling in a different valley from that which we had toiled up almost three months previously. Then all had been brown. Now the hills were green with new grass, the trees were in full leaf, and the green ripening barley blended with the emerald green of wheat and the somber green of potato fields. Unfortunately the fresh food they seemed to promise was not to be had, not even new potatoes. A bundle of young bamboo shoots proved palatable enough but were hardly a luxury, and the seventy rupees demanded was too high a price to pay for a spindly little sheep. Altogether, despite its enticing appearance, Lukhla was one of the least loved of campsites.

The second day out was a bad one. About half an hour from camp, after a late start, we found the coolies waiting at a point where the trail divided into two. After an acrimonious dispute lasting the better part of an hour, the party, to the despair of the sahibs, split into two groups and set off in opposite directions. It turned out that the branches reunited a hundred yards farther on, but so far as tempers were concerned, the rot had set in for the day. Soon the rain started again, a steady drenching deluge falling out of a sullen gray sky. Leeches hung, waving blindly, from every other wayside bush. We picked them off our boots, out of our socks, off the backs of our necks, and the occasional one to break through the defenses and feed itself was singed off, bloated and ugly, to drop on the path in a little explosion of black blood.

We were obliged to stop early that afternoon, already well behind schedule; a laborious crossing of the pass next day in deep snow put us even farther behind. But on the fourth day we began to enjoy our first real break of the whole expedition. The rain had eased during the night and the clouds lifted enough to show the deep, forested gorge of the Inukhu at our feet, the upper slopes red with rhododendrons. We dropped down to the river to a small clearing in the forest for breakfast; slowly the clouds lifted further and a few fitful gleams of sunshine began to break through. Undoubtedly the weather was clearing.

For the rest of the day we climbed steadily beside the river, watching the forest trees growing smaller and giving way to scrub and the country becoming drier, until by mid-afternoon we had reached the little summer village of Lang-sampa, amid the first big yak pastures. It was with some interest that we looked around, for there had been mysterious rumors of an ancient deserted monastery, surrounded by big *mani* walls and with some massive Buddha images above the altar still in place. Obviously the story had improved with the telling. There were *mani* walls to be sure, and a few battered clay images stacked in the corner of a derelict house, but not the grandiose ruins described. Our curiosity satisfied, we turned our attention to the remaining houses of Langsampa. As at the end of any expedition, interest revolved principally around food, and human beings here would presumably be associated with such luxuries as milk, cheese, curd and even, at a price, fresh meat. But despite the fresh traces of a big yak herd, neither man nor beast was to be seen anywhere. The only other village, Thokrak, was an unknown distance upvalley.

"How far to Thokrak?" Jim Wilson asked Hakpanurbu, the Sherpa reputed to be most knowledgeable about the area.

"Fifteen minutes, sahib," came the prompt reply, and he pointed out in the distance the black rock from which he said the little village took its name. Forty minutes' brisk walking and we in the advance party stood gazing over an empty expanse of pasture at a big black rock. Hakpa was puzzled for a moment but rapidly corrected himself. "Some up-sides going, sahib. Some no long. Fifteen minutes." There was no doubting the accuracy of the "up-sides," for ahead the valley was filled by a 300-foot moraine wall with the mountains closing in on either side. We pressed on steadily for an hour or so till a happy cry from Hakpa announced a mob of yaks. A pair of wild-looking Sherpas sat cross-legged on a moraine boulder, eying us cautiously, while a third was loping up a rocky slope in the distance to collect a stray yak.

"How far to Thokrak?" asked Jim for the second time.

Hakpa and the yak men went through the usual ten-minute exchange of ribald conversation that seems essential for a Sherpa to answer such a question.

"Five minutes, sahib," he announced triumphantly.

From behind, a rough New Zealand voice was heard muttering something about "Bloody well heard that one before," but we carried on; the coolies were nowhere in sight but at least food and the mountain were drawing closer. Half an hour later we found ourselves among the few small stone houses of Thokrak—all, alas, empty of both milk and curd. An hour passed, the evening began to darken and grow chill, and the sahibs were regretting their hasty dash to Thokrak, when swaggering into sight came the familiar figure of Pembertarkay, singing lustily. Obviously all was well.

The Lack of a Yak

The only problem next morning was the purchase of a yak. The men of Thokrak proved to be hard bargainers, for even after an hour's blustering and shouting they refused to budge below an astronomical three hundred rupees. Dave Dornan, who held the Kangtega purse, somberly announced that if the yak were bought the remaining cash would be insufficient to pay off the coolies on the return trip. Nevertheless, the "she'll be right" attitude of the yak-steak enthusiasts prevailed and a young female yak (correctly known as a nak) was purchased; given success on the mountain, the bara Sahib was hardly likely to quibble over the odd hundred rupees. Only Angtemba reproachfully

eyed Dornan who was handing over the wad of notes, no
doubt reflecting that the sahibs were casually tossing out
the equivalent of a month's hard-earned wages.

It was now the fifth day, according to schedule the day
on which Base Camp was to be established. Everyone re-
joiced in the first day of perfect weather, for the monsoon
seemed to have faded completely. All day the trail lay up
a lateral moraine trough, moving deeper into a barren mountain landscape. The yak pastures and lakes fell away behind,
the bare ice of the glacier became visible through the moraine, and the jumbled peaks and icefalls of the headwaters
came steadily closer. Still there was no sight of Kangtega,
for the valley swung out east in a wide half circle around
a subsidiary peak obscuring the western portion of the
Mingbo Divide. But just as the two more slothful sahibs in
the rear were contemplating calling a halt, Jim and Dave
returned to announce Kangtega around the corner.

Soon we were sitting together beside a newly erected
cluster of tents, studying the prospect ahead. The head of
the valley was enclosed by a few minor Mingbo summits
scarcely any higher than the terminal névé feeding the
Inukhu glacier. But flanking the névé the peaks were higher.
To the east rose a twin pair of barely climbable 21,000-
footers, while the whole western wall was formed by the
sprawling 22,000-foot Kangtega massif. It seemed hardly
credible that this rather shapeless bulk of snow and ice
was the same peak as that which rose from the Khumbu
in a single sweep of almost vertical rock. Only the summit
cone had any pretensions to steepness; below this final snow
slope a spreading plateau meandered down to disappear
from sight at 21,000 feet, behind a subsidiary rock ridge
screening the unknown middle section of the route. One
assumed that behind this lay a deep snow corridor, for
where the rock ridge fell away the glacier reappeared,
sloping gently south, turned sharply to the right and
plunged into 1500 feet of broken icefall.

The route up the icefall was under discussion when the nak arrived. The Sherpa who brought her up had evidently earned his six rupees, for the nak, unlike its more solemn relative the cow, is a frisky animal, and this one was a mere girl four years old. She'd started the journey with a remarkable display of energy, galloping off with her keeper in full cry behind clinging grimly to the halter; later in the day under the chastening heat of the sun it was the Sherpa who'd done most of the pulling. The whole expedition gathered round admiring the beast, until at last someone turned to Angtemba apologetically and brought up the disagreeable subject of slaughtering the animal. As one, our five Sherpas began to ease their way to the back of the group to discover various essential tasks around the camp. Offers of five rupees' baksheesh produced not a flicker of interest; a ten-rupee note set off a few nervous giggles but no one came forward. It was at this point that Dave Dornan rashly volunteered the assistance of the sahibs; without a word, two of the sahibs sidled off for a closer look at the mountain.

By now the faces of the assembled coolies showed pleased anticipation. It wasn't every day the sahibs turned on a show like this. The nak having been tied down, the onlookers retired to a safe distance, leaving Dornan, myself and the nak eying each other uncomfortably. A breadknife, a blunt kukri and a pair of small surgical scissors formed an improbable collection of weapons of execution, but the sahibs moved in, trying to put a brave face on the matter. After ten minutes' nervous contemplation the kukri was discarded as being too messy and I, as medical officer to the party, stepped forward with the scissors in an attempt to emulate one of the traditional Tibetan methods of yak killing. The thin, sharp blades were pressed hard into the back of the neck, through the hole in the base of the skull and into the brain stem. To the astonishment of everyone present the nak gave a few convulsive kicks, shuddered once or twice, and died. The sinful business of taking life having been concluded, the Sherpas were only too happy to dismember the carcass, and that evening the party dined royally on fillet steaks.

To the Attack

The following day work on the mountain began in earnest. Jim Wilson and I, as reputedly experienced New Zealand ice climbers, deputed to ourselves the task of pushing a route through the icefall, not an easy proposition. The first tentative probe up the northern side soon came to an abrupt halt amidst a network of small but impassable crevasses. Nevertheless it was not an unfruitful move, for now we could see an alternative lead farther south, and an easy one at that, except for a final short section of tangled séracs and slots in the region of the big terminal schrund separating the upper névé-like glacier from the icefall. We scrambled back down towards the foot of the broken section and started up the new line.

Over the first rope length there was a nasty section, a central ice couloir which showed signs of having been swept by a recent ice avalanche; beyond this a small crevassed region, and then we were on a broken but relatively easy slope yielding rapid height. Then we were amongst difficulties again, looking for a way through to the plateau above, now only thirty yards away, with its promise of a fast, easy trip to Camp I. The crevasse blocking the route was an unusually broad and deep one, varying in width and depth along its length and with its architecture distorted in parts by the breaking away from its walls of big curtains of ice, by snow avalanches from above and by the intrusion of the very much more broken and extensive central section of the icefall.

At first we were tempted to try leaping across at a point where the gap narrowed to a slim five feet, but further reflection suggested that a standing broad jump uphill might be more difficult than it looked, especially with a soft-snow takeoff—nor was the prospect of practicing crevasse rescue techniques at 18,000 feet a happy one. For the time being anyway, discretion remained the better part of valor.

The only other alternative was to descend to the floor of the crevasse, which was easy enough, and climb up the opposite wall, which looked exceedingly difficult. The descent was by way of a small natural passage down through the ice to a point where the floor of the crevasse was largely choked by avalanche debris. It was an eerie world down there with the crevasse rapidly deepening on either side, towering walls of polished green ice studded with clusters of icicles, and overhead the long blue strip of sky. Underfoot the avalanche snow felt strangely soft and unstable, as though at any moment the whole of it might suddenly and silently crumple and vanish into the depths below. At its easiest point the opposite wall was feasible, but only just. A leaning drift of soft snow gave a start but above this the ice was gleaming and smooth for fifteen feet before easing off into a shallow gully leading to the plateau above.

Apart from the nak, this was the only real difficulty yet encountered. Jim Wilson accepted the doubtful honor of leading the pitch. Cautiously he moved up the snow lead to the ice, sinking in thigh-deep at each step; suddenly he was sinking very fast straight through the thin soft-snow bridge. Pangboche Tenzing threw his weight on to the belay with commendable speed, but Wilson's outstretched arms and ice ax had already arrested the fall. I was excitedly shooting movie film—an incident at last—while Pembertarkay went to the rescue. There was little doubt that a fair proportion of what they were standing on was merely a thin false floor covering a gaping hole beneath. Wilson tried again, this time treading more carefully. Having solved the problem of his immediate security with a solidly planted ice screw and running belay at head height, he set to work carving a staircase up the wall before him. It was strenuous yet exacting work, requiring considerable delicacy of balance, but at length he had stepped over the rim to the gentle white slopes above. The two Sherpas and I followed quickly, for soon we would have the answer to what the mysterious hidden middle section of the route would have to offer.

It was midafternoon, still blazing hot, and the snow so soft and deep that the only way of making respectable progress was to hand over the job of trail breaking to a Sherpa. Pembertarkay beamed happily, with a "O.K. sahib" resounding enough to set off an avalanche, and started off singing. We had not gone much farther when, topping a small rise, we came into view of the lower half of the northward extension of the glacier. It was much as anticipated: the slopes were gentle, the crevasses few and far between, and the glacier lay deep between containing walls of rock and ice. The day's work was completed, and satisfactorily. But there was one disturbing feature: the slopes were just a little too gentle, considering that they must reach 21,000 feet just around the corner. We turned back with the uneasy feeling that there could well be another icefall hidden up there. Anyway, provided this miraculous weather held, we would have the answer on the morrow.

Dave and Tom had shifted Base Camp up to the foot of the icefall during the day in preparation for the big carry to Camp I next day. The prospect of pushing up the upper slopes of the glacier was not one to fill the party with joy, for undoubtedly the whole lot would be knee-deep in soft snow once the sun had thawed the frozen surface. To gain as much height as possible during the cool of the early morning, breakfast was ordered for the early hours, any time after midnight. The Sherpas, too, approved of the scheme and as a result all were on the move at five o'clock next morning. Yesterday's trail was easily followed and we moved fast; but the sun moved faster, climbing inexorably above the eastern peaks and shining down into the great snow corridor up which the route now lay. Hour by hour the sun climbed higher, beating mercilessly down on the hapless nine struggling upwards in the ever softening snow. There was no escape from it, not a single oasis of shade in a white world of trembling heat. The Sherpas had least trouble, despite their forty-pound loads. The sahibs, breaking trail in front and route finding among the crevasses, were less happy. Forebodings about a second icefall seemed all too likely to be justified, for after a brief rise in the central section of the glacier, it had flattened out again, with ominous ice cliffs appearing high on the left. The glacier lay in a deep steep-walled valley, which, as the Sherpas were quick to point out, was strikingly like a smaller version of the Everest Western Cwm. It was after midday when the exhausted party moved round the final bend in the glacier to come face to face with the final unknown section of the route. It was steep, yes, and there was a single big side-to-side schrund; but there was also almost certainly a route through. Given good weather and sufficient strength—this was the seventh day now without a rest—we felt sure we could reach the summit.

Camp I was established at 20,300 feet on the level névé below the schrund. An early start was planned for next morning, as for the carry up from Base Camp. But the weather decreed otherwise; at the appointed hour of two o'clock the silence of the night was broken by the whispering patter of snow falling on the tents. Outside the stars had vanished and the air thickened with mist, and the tracks around the tents were disappearing under a blanket of fine "sago" snow. It looked as though the monsoon had crept back just when the summit was within striking distance. Barely a word was said as we four climbers slunk back into our sleeping bags to wait for daylight.

At six o'clock, though the mist still hung around, the

snow had stopped. The day had hardly dawned promisingly, but even the smallest reprieve was welcomed; by the time we had completed a solid breakfast of rice and nak steaks the mist in the cwm had lifted a little, revealing a sky filled with lowering gray clouds. We set off in the direction of the big schrund, which looked less and less easy the closer it was approached. The general atmosphere was one of depression, resulting from the uncertainty of the weather and the exhaustion of the previous day. And let it be admitted, enthusiasm for the summit was tempered to some extent by the daunting prospect of 2000 feet of plugging in deep snow.

At length a snow bridge of sorts was found. The party roped in two pairs, Wilson and I leading, Dornan and Frost behind. Beyond the first big schrund the crevasses presented no difficulties, except for the maddening deviations they imposed on the route. And now began five hours of suffering on the interminable upper snow plateau. In the snow conditions our worst fears were realized, for it was breakable crust overlying knee-deep snow, a nightmare to climbers even at low altitude. More and more we began to realize how badly we needed a rest day. Frost, with less experience at high altitude than the rest of us, was making heavy weather of the trail and had to be nursed along by Dornan. Jim and I seemed in slightly better shape but soon began to slow down under the frustrating, infuriating labor imposed on us by the conditions. We began to count steps —150 carefully placed footprints, then step to the side for the change of lead; and when this was too much it became 100 each. At intervals the clouds came down, blanking out the scene in brief flurries of snow and filling the line of tracks; we began to wonder seriously whether we could make it.

But at length the foot of the 800-foot summit cone was reached. It was shortly after noon when I started up the first rope length, wondering uneasily what the snow would

53. The 22,360-foot Kangtega presents a dominant, menacing façade above Thyangboche monastery

54. Over the yak pass leading into the forested gorge named Inukhu

55. 17,000 feet up Kangtega, Base Camp was established at foot of icefall

56. Brighter prospects seen from Inukhu: a single relatively easy icefall guards
the gently rising glacier

57. Porters approach the main icefall

58. Last few feet of Kangtega, showing breakaway of second avalanche

59. At the top: Dave Dornan hails members below

be like; the angle of the slope was similar to that of the summit slopes of Taweche or Ama Dablam—given the almost bottomless soft rubbish encountered on Taweche, the peak would be impossible; easy chipping in firm snow, as on Ama Dablam, and probably we'd make it. With sinking spirits I floundered upwards, leaving a deep trench behind me, and the situation was made gloomier still by a change for the worse in the weather. My enthusiasm is notably easily dampened by bad weather. The change prompted me to question the wisdom of going on.

"We're going to the top," from Dornan was the only reply from the trio below.

Then the whole complexion of the climb changed. As I reached the upper lip of the terminal schrund I was able to start work with my ice ax; three scrapes, a kick, and there was a neat, solid little pigeonhole of a step in crisp snow. Now we were gaining height fast. With solid shaft belays giving complete security, a snow staircase rising easily at fifty degrees, and no avalanche danger, we moved quickly to the upper schrund, 200 feet below the summit. The schrund itself presented no real difficulty, but above it there were two routes to choose between. The first was by way of the gentle but corniced summit ridge; the second was a continuation of the face we had just climbed but lay farther to the right, directly below the top. Despite its uncompromising angle, we decided on the second alternative, because of its presumed freedom from the soft snow and dangerous cornices.

Avalanche!

It was an unfortunate choice that nearly ended in disaster. Jim led off and at first found good crisp snow as expected. But then it began to soften and the steps broke away. Curse and fume at it as we would, the anger of a tiny, exhausted human was no help against the massive indifference of this mountain; only patient kicking and plowing could find a way up here. Jim had reached a point twenty feet short of the summit when a brief, sharp "phrumph" came from above, the ominous precursor to the breaking away of a soft-snow avalanche. In the white yielding surface of the snow just above him, a thin semicircular crack had opened up.

Eying it uneasily, he dug down to a harder surface below for a shaft belay and called me up to join him.

It was a dangerous situation. Whereas the lower slopes had been blown clear by the wind, up here there had been enough lee protection to allow four feet of new snow to collect over an underlying hard surface. In the hills at home we would immediately have retreated from such a situation; but by now we were all affected by the indifference bred of exhaustion and there was a hint of desperation in our determination to win those last few rope lengths.

Jim had a fair sort of belay and the other pair were not in the line which presumably an avalanche would take. I started on the final pitch. Immediately I found myself flailing into a seemingly bottomless morass of soft snow. Slowly a deep trench-like trail opened behind me.

And then there was a smooth "swish," and almost silently a foot of snow peeled off from below the line of steps as though sliced off with a knife.

"Hang on a minute," Jim called out grimly, "and I'll dig down to a better belay."

As yet the bigger part of the potential avalanche remained poised, above and between the two of us. An "O.K." came up from below and I started again. Only ten feet to go.

Then suddenly a terrifying crunch cut the air. This one was *big*. I plunged my ice ax deep into the snow, burying my arms to the shoulder. From the corner of my eye I could see a curling white wave surging down the mountain like the foaming crest of a comber on an ocean beach. Grimly I waited for Wilson's weight to come on to the makeshift belay.

Meanwhile, farther down the slope, Jim had thrown his weight forward onto his belay, head down, while the surging snow ran over and around him. Equally grimly he waited for my seemingly inevitable fall.

But the dust settled, the silence returned and we found we were all still safe on the mountain. A glance below showed that the avalanche had swept past Dornan and Frost, who were dug in and expecting the worst. The sliding mass of snow had no more than brushed them.

There still remained a shingle thin slab of snow above Wilson, but even if this went it was small enough not to be dangerous. I crawled to the crest of the ridge to find that I was on a big cornice overhanging the incredible precipice forming the north wall of Kangtega's High Peak. Menaced to both north and south, I hastily turned east to a more solid-looking ice bulge and belayed Wilson up to join me. The summit was still thirty feet away and perhaps three feet vertically above the point where we stood, but so far as we were concerned this was near enough to the top. The summit of Kangtega was not a healthy-looking spot, nor was there any view; and besides, the traverse would almost certainly precipitate the remaining avalanche on top of Dornan and Frost. With no regrets we cut quickly down past the other pair to the schrund, the snow bridge across it consolidated by the addition of a few tons of fresh avalanche snow.

Tom had vomited after eating some food and now was experiencing the sensations of some of the more advanced stages of exhaustion, in the unique forms known only to devotees of high-altitude climbing. He stumbled upwards, his pallid features expressing disgust at the rotten snow and breaking steps. The only climbing talents needed here were determination and brute strength—it was a far cry back to the delicate, airy acrobatics of rock-climbing on the big sun-drenched walls of Yosemite.

Summit

With Jim and me out of the line of fire, Dave was free to complete the traverse to the summit—a move which, as predicted, sent the third avalanche rumbling off to join its fellows. It was about four o'clock when Dave stepped onto the highest point of Kangtega to become, technically, the only member of the party to reach the summit. Dimly through the mist he could distinguish the outline of the Low Peak and enough of the details to be confident that it was easily accessible from where he stood; it was confirmation of what had seemed probable from the Khumbu and set to rest fears that the major challenge of Kangtega had not been met.

The descent passed with remarkable ease and speed, for the tracks were easily picked up and the whole route was downhill. Back at Camp I we brewed quantities of tea, hot jelly, and various other liquids, and the yak-steak enthusiasts devoured what was left of the meat. Someone mooted the improbable idea that the sahibs should carry the camp down next day. Predictably, such foolishness was not discussed further, and the next morning was far advanced before anyone began to stir feebly. A glance outside showed that the weather had not broken, for the sun was blazing from a clear sky. The atmosphere was growing more and more oppressive, when drifting up through the noon heat came a familiar sound. It was Pembertarkay singing. Five black dots appeared over the rim of the névé and soon they were up to the camp, shaking hands with us and as pleased as we were. With the remarkably acute sight common to most Sherpas, they had picked out the tracks leading to the summit, both of us and the avalanches. It seemed a pity that no Sherpa had had the chance to go to the top—particularly Angtemba, who had done magnificient work on Taweche and Kangtega, both as sirdar and climber—but there just hadn't been sufficient time.

Most Important Part of the Climb

The summit day had been a memorable one, not least remarkable being the fact that it had been the eighth day out from Khumjung, exactly as planned. It seemed strange that this, the most fearsome-looking of the Khumbu peaks, should have yielded so easily, but it confirmed an aphorism that any Himalayan party might well bear in mind: the most important part of the climb is finding the right route. There was food for thought, too, in what exactly had been achieved. The summit, certainly—and this for the press, who eagerly trumpeted the news abroad—was all that mattered; whereas the climb on Taweche, which was technically a far greater achievement, was mentioned only to be dismissed as a failure. Of pleasure there had been precious little on the mountain; all four of us would have agreed that this agonizing struggle was scarcely comparable with the delights of climbing on our chosen peaks in Yosemite and the Tetons in the United States, or the Southern Alps of New Zealand. Yet there remained those few precious moments resting in the memory, the splendid desolation of a Himalayan panorama, the drifting mist, the spasms of fear, the silence of a great white névé under a gray sky—these are the hard-earned, priceless moments that remain when the pain and exhaustion have faded into oblivion. These are the justifications.

—Mike Gill

Chapter 10

"YOU WILL COME BACK!"

It was now early June and the various programs were nearly completed. Our Sherpa friends realized we would soon be returning home and for a few giddy days opened their hearts to us.

It started with breakfast at Annullu's. As we approached his house in the crisp air of early morning, we noticed a brazier of incense burning beside the door, filling the atmosphere with pungent perfume. Inside were gathered many of the important men of the district. The head lama was there with other important lamas, Dawa Tenzing, the various headmen of Khumjung and Namche Bazar, and many other senior Sherpas. We were led to seats of honor and, despite the early hour, welcomed with glasses of fine rice chang. On the table were bowls of rhododendrons and the glass-filled windows framed a tremendous view of Kangtega and Ama Dablam. Chang on an empty stomach works wonders and we were soon a loud and noisy group. Breakfast was a sumptuous meal. American boned turkey, American one-minute rice, local spinach, and wonderful potato chips and fried eggs. At the end we had large mugs of American cocoa —no wonder the American Everest Expedition were complaining about their lack of food when we saw them in Namche Bazar.

Most Khumjung houses had their little stock of expedition luxuries, some obtained quite honestly but much acquired illicitly. Yet I imagine that few parties in this area have suffered the same amount of pillaging as this American expedition. It had been our observation that the teams of porters who came down from Base Camp to obtain local food rarely came down with empty rucksacks. Pillaging will always occur on an expedition unless discipline is maintained both by the sahibs and the Sherpa sirdar. The Americans had adopted the system of dividing the authority among three sirdars, and the Khumjung Sherpas all agreed that this had not worked successfully. The resultant conflict and jealousy had produced a lessening of personal responsibility.

Father and Mother of the Village

Annullu's breakfast was enlivened by many stories of heroic efforts on the mountains—and in true Sherpa fashion none of these stories suffered in the telling. It was a noisy and convivial party but it was climaxed with a dignified little ceremony. Annullu raised his hand for silence and then made a short speech. We had, he said, lightened their darkness, saved their lives, and eased their domestic problems. We were indeed the father and mother of the village.

Even allowing for a lot of exaggeration, it was clear that our expedition efforts had been well appreciated.

In a happy group we drifted down to the school where Khunjo Chumbi had arranged some Tibetan dancing for us. Placed upright in the ground was a huge pole, supported by long ropes, on which we were to see acrobatics. The head lama sat cross-legged on a high place in front of the school with all his satellites around him, and we had seats nearby. The dancers were professionals and very expert, but despite the colorful costuming the program became rather stylized and long-winded. K. C., between bursts of laughter, kept describing what it all meant. The first major dance involved three princesses, a brave young prince and a "haunting man." Another was all about warriors and decapitations, and the villain laid about so enthusiastically with his vicious sword that we expected to see blood spurting at any moment. Finally the acrobat arrived and flung himself around in wild circles. Groups of men clung to the steadying ropes as he clambered up the long pole and postured and danced on top with remarkable balance and vigor. By the reaction of the crowd this was terribly funny, so we asked K. C. what it all meant. He was able only to mumble something about "man and woman" before being overcome with laughter.

To the disappointment of everyone it started raining, and we retreated to our camp and entertained the head lama to the usual lunch—soup, potatoes and pancakes. There was no doubt that the head lama enjoyed our company. With us he was always relaxed and cheerful and seemed less like a reincarnate and more like a human being. Someone asked him where he had been born, but he just laughed and said he didn't know—a Rimpoche's spirit has been in the world for many years and in many bodies, so his actual physical birth doesn't count.

As the rain persisted, Khunjo organized dancing by the Tibetans in the Khumjung schoolhouse. This was much more fun. The six giant men with vivid red hats and long turquoise earrings swung and stamped until the whole building shuddered. At the end they sang a song honoring each one of us personally and gave each of us a scarf. We finally parted with much bowing and salaaming.

The day was to conclude with dinner at Mingmatserings. We arrived rather late at Khunde to find his house magnificently decorated for the occasion. All his best rugs covered the benches, and the tables were draped with green plastic. For cocktails we had fine rice chang and some expedition crackers and cheese. But dinner was a real Tibetan meal. Piles of *tukpa* (handmade noodles) and a lovely thin soup were handed to us in dainty Chinese bowls. We put the tukpa into the soup and added a mixture of chopped yak, spring onion and butter. As the yak was fresh, this proved a very tasty repast, and it was washed down most pleasantly with Mingma's good home-brew.

Afterwards we had the usual songs and speeches. At the appropriate moment we produced our gifts—a Norwegian jersey for Mingma, a bottle of scent and some pale-yellow pearls for Mrs. Mingma, and an embroidered handkerchief for the old mother. Alas, the old lady could hardly see her present. Two years ago she had been tall, straight and handsome but now she was toothless and nearly blind. It seemed sad for this degeneration to have happened so quickly but it is an inevitable consequence of the hard life the Sherpa women lead.

The Khunde Major, who is senior headman of both Khumjung and Khunde villages, asked us to visit him after dinner to celebrate his daughter's recent engagement. We walked to his house along narrow, walled paths, crept past the two giant mastiffs guarding his door, and climbed up the internal stairway in pitch-darkness. In the living room everything was bright and sparkling. The major's home is the first one in the area to have a chimney and, as befitted such a rich and influential man, his walls were lined with row after row of magnificent copperware—all gleaming in the smoke-free atmosphere. His beautiful daughter-in-law served chang in delicate Chinese dishes with daintily worked silver stands.

Suddenly the major and Kunjo Chumbi decided to dance. They leaped to their feet and swung into rhythm. Kunjo's footwork was extremely vigorous and his stamping absolutely brilliant despite his fifty-six years. He waved his long loose sleeves in traditional manner, and his pleated bakhu swung most rhythmically. All the neighbors started to appear, including a handsome young Tibetan nobleman refugee with a Tibetan guitar. Tall and debonair, with plaited hair tied round his head, he wore a silk mandarin-collared shirt and took his wind jacket off one shoulder so it swung in nonchalant style down his back. He led the dancers into action, plucking at his instrument with great verve, and the whole room became full of movement and color. The footwork became faster and more intricate and the concentration of the dancers almost hypnotic. Round and round they swirled for hour after hour, and when Mingma discreetly gave us the sign to leave they hardly noticed our departure. We walked back to camp in white moonlight, still drifting on a cloud of warmth and melody.

Khumbu Farewells

Our last task before leaving Khumjung was a quick visit to Pangboche to check school progress and say our goodbyes. The head lama had insisted we stay at Thyangboche. When we walked up the 2000 feet from the Dudh Kosi River we found him waiting to escort us to the new rest house. A week before, I had given him one of the simple expedition wood-burning stoves and this was now glowing in the main living room, taking all the chill out of the air. Our quarters had been prepared with special care. The chairs were covered with bright carpet squares, while our beds were a mass of soft Tibetan rugs. On a little table was a handsome bowl filled with flowers. We were given the traditional tea and chang, but this was followed by more substantial fare in the form of dahi, tsampa, and some American canned date loaf.

The head lama told us of his plans for the further development of the rest house—a terrace and a protecting rock wall and, best of all, a flower garden. When we had finished our meal and were warm and rested, he invited us to accompany him on a tour of inspection. He conducted us to the edge of the cliff and showed us his particular pride, the new toilet. He opened the door with a flourish and beckoned us all in. What a scene met our eyes! A wooden platform with a sheltering roof had been built out over the rhododendron forest, and there were two friendly little holes cut in the floor. Two thousand feet below, the Dudh Kosi foamed through its narrow gorge. It would be necessary to watch your step here if you were to return from the toilet alive.

At Pangboche School there was a welcoming arch and two lines of shining-faced children—fifty-four of them. The school was showing the signs of careful attention by teacher Phutenzi. He had already planted primulas on top of the courtyard walls and had sown potatoes in a corner of waste ground. We sat and watched the children at classes and marveled at the improvement in two short months. The proud parents provided chang, tea and scarves, and I made a speech.

Lunch was down in the village in the house we had rented for the Phorche children. Phutenzi's room seemed very comfortable and the thirteen Phorche children were well established. Mothers from Phorche were taking turns coming up to mind the children and everything seemed very well and happily organized. We left Pangboche feeling that a profitable school year lay ahead of the children.

Foreign Aid and Domestic Aides

What is the future of work like ours in the Khumbu? The Nepalese Government has told us they plan within five years to take over our schools and operate them within the national education framework. This would be the ideal conclusion to our efforts. Even if it doesn't immediately eventuate, I'm sure money can be found somehow to keep the schools going. The Khumjung School has had many side effects—not the least is the way it has stimulated the government into opening schools itself. Namche Bazar, Chaunrikharka and Junbesi now officially have been appointed government schools and an annual grant of Rs 800 ($106) made to each of them to pay for a teacher and running costs. Such a sum is barely adequate even in the warm temperatures of the lowlands of Nepal, but up in Solu Khumbu it is clearly insufficient. The rigorous climate demands more clothes, food is more expensive, and firewood is needed for heating. The result is that at the moment only one of these schools is operating—in a halfhearted fashion.

The world-wide shortage of good teachers is nowhere more apparent than in Nepal, where the school system is only a few years old. Most of the country teachers are Nepalese boys who have just completed their high school courses and are looking desperately for work that will not involve physical labor. They have no teacher training, little real knowledge and no discipline. We have tried to overcome this initially by importing teachers from the mountain areas of Darjeeling and Kalimpong in Northern India—teachers who have been well trained in the good schools around Darjeeling—and this has proved highly successful. But though our teachers are of Sherpa birth and speak Nepali as their mother tongue, yet they are not readily accepted by the Nepalese Government, which regards them still basically as Indians—and Indians are always suspect in Nepal, however worthy they may be.

Realizing this problem, we hope to overcome it by developing teachers out of our own schools. Already one of our five teachers, Kalden Sherpa, is a local boy, and we plan to give other outstanding pupils the opportunity to go on with their studies and train to become teachers. One generous American suggested we send several of the brighter boys to the United States, give them a thorough schooling, and then bring them back as teachers. Such a plan would be doomed to failure and would in fact only do harm to the Sherpa community. There is so little in common in standards of comfort, hygiene, entertainment, food and even local customs between a Sherpa village and an American city that although the students might well adapt to the latter, they would lose all interest in returning to the discomforts of the former. A teacher whose thoughts are eternally turned to what might have been isn't of much use in a pioneer community—or anywhere else for that matter. It would be much better to import a few dedicated Western teachers who could impart their knowledge and discipline to the pupils without disturbing too much their sense of involvement as part of the village community life. The aim of our schools must be to help the Sherpas overcome the unnecessary discomforts, ill health, poverty and ignorance which are present in every village—not to encourage a mass migration to the warmer lowlands. The Sherpas' finest traits have been developed in their battle against their tough environment. The last thing I would wish to do is to remove them from battle completely; better to put some sharper weapons into the Sherpas' hands.

Already I am making plans to return again to Solu Khumbu. There is a little plateau of land at Chaunrikharka protruding into the uncompromising steepness of the Dudh Kosi Valley. It should be possible to construct a thousand-foot-long airfield on it—long enough for the redoubtable Pilatus Porter to use even at this altitude. An airfield only a day's march from Khumjung would allow easier support and supervision of the schools and would also make it much simpler for the Nepalese Government to develop this region.

The "shadow" schools at Namche Bazar, Chaunrikharka and Junbesi need urgent assistance to become schools in fact. We will construct buildings, supply equipment and help out with teachers. There are still many people in Solu Khumbu who haven't been vaccinated against smallpox, so we'll try hard to get to all of them. And perhaps someday I'll be able to achieve my ambition of a small hospital at Khumjung.

We said goodbye to the head lama in his exquisite room in the Thyangboche Monastery. I was overwhelmed to receive an ancient monastery book—in raised gold script on dark-green paper—and a long silk scarf blessed by the lama himself.

"You will come back," he said, nodding his head with firm conviction. "You have seen the sun rise on the sacred summit of Khumbila.

"You will come back!"

Down from Shangri-La

Early on June 7 we pulled down the last of our tents and made ready for departure. Louise describes our last few hours:

"As we finished breakfast various villagers arrived in their best clothes, clutching bottles of chang and rakshi. Soon a marvelous ceremony and general leave-taking were underway. Many of the senior members of the community had been doing a puja at the gompa which included a vow of silence, but the head lama had given them a special dispensation to break their vow for our departure. They were all in bare feet with white and scarlet silk scarves over their heads, carrying their prayer wheels. The day became gloriously sunny and all our many friends made us drink their particular farewell drink, so that at times I had two glasses in my hands which were being constantly refilled with various thick, lumpy vintages. There was no point in worrying about an upset stomach—after all you don't often have a whole village turn out with their individual containers of chang to see you off. Nima Dorje and his mother came and made us drink and gave us scarves and a Tibetan calendar. Then Annullu and his wife and their children. Also Kuncha and his very handsome and dignified father. Ongchu Lama and his wife appeared with rakshi and scarves and a little religious picture for me—and so it went, on and on.

Then we had our farewell at the school.

All the children were sitting cross-legged on the playground and we sat at the table, having more chang and tea. Ang Rita, the class leader, stood up and made a speech and handed it to Ed. It was all rather charming, but as we handed round scarves to the masters and said our goodbyes to the school children I felt a terrible emotional tension rising. I walked out of the school gates to find Mrs. Mingma and her two little boys. I shook her hand and, as is the delightful custom in these parts with someone that you particularly like, she put my hand to her forehead. She looked so sad that the two of us just broke down and embraced each other with tears pouring down our cheeks. It was terrible after that—all my special women friends had watery eyes and the men too, and saying our final goodbyes I thought I would burst. Thank God most people were weeping, so I didn't feel so bad.

Ed and Desmond had faces as grim as death. Everyone followed us to the village gateway, a sorrowful, silent crowd.

As we at last started up the track to Namche, I let out a burst of emotion and at that altitude could hardly breathe. I tried to talk to Ed and Desmond but they were having their own problems and wouldn't look at me.

Suddenly the tension broke—down below us the school children started cheering and all the villagers took up the cry. We smiled with relief and looked down at all our many friends standing on the Khumjung Maidan with that little Shangri-La village behind, its green crops flourishing, its sturdy snug little houses—and the towering snowy mountains behind."

ROSTER OF THE EXPEDITION

The scientists, specialists, and mountaineers who accompanied Sir Edmund Hillary on the Himalayan Schoolhouse Expedition 1963 were:

Bhanu Bannerjee
Interpreter and Newspaper Photographer
Bengal, India

Desmond Doig
Assistant Editor, *The Statesman*
Calcutta and New Delhi, India

David Dornan
Candidate for M.A. in Philosophy
University of Colorado

Murray Ellis
Engineer
New Zealand

Tom Frost
Aeronautical Engineer
U.S.A.

Dr. Michael Gill
Physician
New Zealand

Dr. Phillip Houghton
Physician
New Zealand

Jim Wilson
M.A. in Philosophy
New Zealand

They were later joined by

Doreen Del Fium
Geologist
Los Angeles, California

Ann Wilson
Nurse and artist

Louise Hillary

Ralph Wyeth
U.N.-appointed General Manager
Nepal Bank, Katmandu

GLOSSARY

Bakhu – long flowing robe worn by Sherpas and Tibetans

Baksheesh – payment, in addition to regular wages, for special labor or service

Belay – the act of securing the climber's rope around a projecting rock, a steel spike, or an ice ax sunk deeply in the snow

Bergschrund – a type of crevasse usually separating a static snow slope from a moving glacier

Carabiner – metal snaplink for attaching ropes together or for belaying points

Chang – a beer, often with the consistency of thick gruel, which the Sherpas make from the grain of the millet grass

Chapatties – flat, unleavened bread made from flour and water

Chorten – a Buddhist religious monument normally covering some holy relics

Couloir – steep gully of rock or snow

Crampons – metal frames with ten or twelve sharp spikes. They can be strapped to the sole of a climbing boot to give a firm grip on ice or hard snow.

Dahi – curds

Dhal – split peas

Garam pani and sawun – hot water and soap

Ghat – a river crossing, or place for the cremation of the dead

Ghee – cooking fat

Glissade – a sliding descent of a snow slope

Gompa – Buddhist temple

Kata – the traditional white scarf used in Tibetan Buddhist ceremonies or to honor and welcome a visitor

Khumbila – god of the Solu Khumbu Sherpas

Kukri – heavy long knife used in Nepal

Namaste – term of greeting

Névé – the source snow field at the head of a glacier

Panchyat – village council

Pitons – metal spikes of varying lengths and shapes to be driven into cracks in the rock or into ice. They have an eye at one end to which a carabiner can be attached to hold a safety rope.

Puja – Buddhist rite including fasting and special prayer

Rakshi – Sherpa name for a spirituous drink distilled usually from potatoes, rice or various grains

Rappelling – lowering yourself on a doubled rope down steep cliffs

Rupee – Nepalese monetary unit equivalent to about 14 cents, U.S. currency

Sérac – a tower of ice usually in a glacier, often unstable and dangerous

Schrund – a short form of bergschrund

Sherpa – name of the people living mostly above 7000 feet on the south side of the Himalayan range. They originally came from Tibet, are of Mongolian origin, Mahayana Buddhist religion, and Nepalese nationality.

Sirdar – foreman of the gang (not only Sherpa)

Tsampa – cooked ground barley

Tukpa – handmade noodles

Yeti – the Sherpa name for the mysterious creature called by Westerners the "Abominable Snowman"